STARTING SCHOOL

Dr Richard Woolfson

Thorsons
An Imprint of HarperCollins*Publishers*

Thorsons
An Imprint of HarperCollins*Publishers*
77–85 Fulham Palace Road,
Hammersmith, London W6 8JB
1160 Battery Street,
San Francisco, California 94111-1213

Published by Thorsons 1995

10 9 8 7 6 5 4 3 2 1

© Richard Woolfson 1995

Richard Woolfson asserts the moral right to
be identified as the author of this work

A catalogue record for this book
is available from the British Library

ISBN 0 7225 3100 1

Printed in Great Britain by
HarperCollinsManufacturing, Glasgow

Text cartoons by Harry Venning

TO ELLIOT, NAOMI AND GEMMA

Contents

Acknowledgements   vii
Introduction   ix

PART I—LAYING THE FOUNDATIONS (0–3 YEARS)
Chapter 1:   Changes in Development from Birth to 3   3

PART II—TIME FOR PRE-SCHOOL
Chapter 2:   Nursery or Playgroup (3 Years +)   15

PART III—FROM PRE-SCHOOL TO INFANT SCHOOL
Chapter 3:   Readiness for School   25

PART IV—THRIVING IN INFANT SCHOOL
Chapter 4:   Personality Counts   43
Chapter 5:   Encouraging Your Child's Independence   58
Chapter 6:   Learning in the Classroom   72
Chapter 7:   The 'Three Rs'   88

PART V—THE 'RIGHT' INFANT SCHOOL
Chapter 8:   Choosing an Infant School   105

PART VI—STARTING INFANT SCHOOL
Chapter 9:   Countdown to the First Day   119
Chapter 10:   The First Day   125

PART VII—PROBLEMS IN SCHOOL
Chapter 11:   When Things Go Wrong   139
Chapter 12:   Children with Special Needs   160

Useful Addresses   175
Index   177

ACKNOWLEDGEMENTS

Thanks to Sarah Sutton for help in preparing the final manuscript, and to Lisa, Tessa and Eve for their love and encouragement.

INTRODUCTION

Starting school is such a big step. Even in today's era of sophistication, it is unrealistic to expect any young child to develop spontaneously the skills and strategies needed to cope with school. Your child is no different in this respect. Your child needs your advice, your support and your planning, to ensure school becomes a place associated with enjoyment, not stress, a place associated with learning, not fear, a place associated with success, not failure. That's how to give your child a headstart, so that your child's potential is fully maximized.

Starting School isn't a recipe book for guaranteeing that beginning in the infant class will go smoothly, without any teething troubles. But it does point out the potential pitfalls, advises you on how these can be avoided, and offers many positive practical suggestions for things you can do during the pre-school years to help your child to be ready for this new life phase. This can only be a positive step for you to take.

1

LAYING THE FOUNDATIONS
(0–3 YEARS)

CHANGES IN DEVELOPMENT FROM BIRTH TO 3

School, for most children, starts around the age of 5 years. But the process of preparing your child for school starts long before that—it starts the moments she arrives into this world.

No one is suggesting, of course, that you start 'grooming' her for school life at such a young age; yet there is no doubt that the way you raise your child in these crucial early years has a great influence on her subsequent development and achievements during the pre-school years. That's why this book devotes these first chapters to the early part of your child's life. At each stage of her growth, your child needs your supervision, guidance and support, so that she can reach her full potential.

DEVELOPMENTAL CHANGES

The chart below lists the major developmental changes that occur in the first 3 years of your child's life:

Age Range	Developmental Changes during this Period
0–12 months	From birth onwards she becomes fascinated by the world around her.
	Birth weight doubles by the age of 5 months and triples by 12 months. Length increases from around 20 in (50 cm) at birth to over 30 in (80 cm) a year later.
	From having little control over her limbs at birth, at 12 months she can control her head and arm movements.
	By one year, she can reach out for objects and can sit up independently.
	By 12 months, she focuses longer on specific people or objects that catch her attention.
	Your baby begins to enjoy routines such as bedtime or bathtime. She looks forward to them.
12–24 months	Compared to a young baby, she's much bigger, heavier and less fragile in appearance.
	Growth is slower, but she will gain roughly 5 lb (2.25 kg) in weight this year.
	Length also increases, as she becomes around 5 in (12.5 cm) taller.
	Your toddler's pot belly is partly due to her under-developed stomach muscles.
	The second year is also marked by your child's ability to walk—hence the term 'toddler'.
	Being more independent, she can voyage into new territory without your help.

Your infant's natural curiosity increases, as she learns new things every day.

24–36 months   Weight gain is around 5 lb (2.25 kg), and she gains in height by around 4 in (10 cm).

All 20 primary teeth emerge, so she can chew foods more effectively.

Your child becomes very difficult and demanding, especially if she doesn't get her own way.

Temper tantrums are common at this age—2-year-olds can be very difficult and moody.

Changes in your child's understanding of herself make her feel self-important.

She doesn't like rules (except her own) and may fight against them.

She does not yet play cooperatively, but she tries to be sociable.

PLAY IN THE PRE-SCHOOL YEARS

For adults, the very word 'play' suggests a leisure pursuit with the sole purpose of providing relaxation and amusement. For children, however, play is much more important. Play is your child's way of interacting with the world around her; play is her way of learning; play is her way of expressing her feelings; play is her way of mixing with other children her own age; and play is her way discovering her own capabilities.

When she is **one month**, you will see plenty of occasions when she shakes her rattle, bangs the side of her cot, chews her hand, bites the mattress, and so on. She does this to learn about objects that she can see and touch. Only by exploring, touching, looking, and even tasting can she acquire knowledge at this age. She cannot talk and she cannot ask you questions, so getting hands-on contact with anything within her reach is her way of connecting with the outside world. Your baby's cot must be a place for activity, not just for sleep, because she spends a lot of time in it. The fun she has from exploring is sufficient incentive for her to continue with it.

Although your child cannot speak at the age of **six months**, she still enjoys language play. She babbles consistently – maybe her sounds make sense to her, even if they are unintelligible to you. Music becomes important to her as well. You may find that her face brightens up when she recognizes a familiar jingle playing on the radio; and that she starts to make animated body movements when she hears her favourite tune, as though she is intuitively trying to dance. She will happily fall asleep to the sound of you singing her a lullaby, whereas your older children may cringe when they hear your voice.

Things change by the time she is **12 months**. She is no longer rooted to the one spot. She crawls actively around the floor, rolls over from her front to back, and is generally more active. This mobility means your infant does not have to wait for the world to come to her – she can start to move by herself. Although at this age she cannot go exactly where she wants, she can at least try. Soon she will be walking around the house without your help, then running, and within a couple of years she will be much more agile. A whole new array of opportunities opens up to your child as a result of these new physical skills – no wonder she enjoys it and wants to keep on the move the whole time.

At the age of **18 months** she begins to become fascinated by puzzles – though bear in mind that to your infant, anything can be a puzzle. For instance, a box with a lid on it, or a sweet that is wrapped up in paper, is a problem she wants to solve. You have probably wondered why you bother buying her a toy at all because she usually shows more interest in the packaging! And her little hands have an amazing capacity to explore. Shape-sorters are particularly popular at this age; the combination of the bright colours, coupled with the challenge of putting the right shape in the right hole, makes it very enticing for your little explorer.

At **2 years** her play takes on a new dimension. You might find her pretending to drink out of a cup that is empty, or giving teddy a very serious reprimand. Her imagination has begun to develop and, in her mind, she can turn anything into whatever she wants or make any cuddly toy become alive. Of course, her pretend play at this age is very basic, but it does develop. And the great thing about this type of play, as far as your infant is concerned, is that she is totally in control. She does not need you to buy her that train set because she can 'make' the train from any object that she wants. Later on she realizes that she can dress up and pretend to be someone else.

Young children around the age of **30 months** love splashing about with paint, or drawing completely unrecognizable pictures with crayons. As well as providing another medium for expressing and developing imagination, this type of play is a useful way for improving your child's control over her hands and fingers. Do not expect a child of this age to be neat when she is painting; make sure she has got on old clothes or an apron. She wants you to take an interest in her sketches, perhaps even for you to put one or two up on the kitchen wall.

Your child will thoroughly enjoy playing with other children when she is around **3 years** old. This year sees a rapid transformation in your child's ability to mix properly with her friends. Naturally they do argue now and again, but if you watch them playing you will notice that there are many more occasions when they are together without any bickering. Your child is able to play this way because she is more mature, and realizes that her friends have feelings too. She is more caring and aware of others.

ACTION PLAN FOR ENCOURAGING YOUR CHILD'S DEVELOPMENT: 0–12 MONTHS

1. **Speak to her.** Your baby just adores you talking to her, even though she cannot answer you back in words. But she does answer you with big wide eyes and a very winning smile – this is proof that she likes your attention and she wants you to continue speaking to her.

2. **Give her lots to catch her interest.** Although she spends time during the day lying on her back in the cot, there is still plenty of potential for play. Try to ensure that she has toys lying beside her that she can reach, and something hanging from the ceiling to attract her attention.

3. **Don't just watch.** You probably love observing your young baby at play, and she enjoys your attention too. But there is no harm in joining in with her. Hold the fluffy ball and tantalizingly tickle her little fingers, or simply shake the rattle as you pass it to her. You do not need to be passive.

4. **Pick toys that you think she will enjoy, not toys that look good.** During this first year of life, she will always be attracted to a toy that is in one of the primary colours and that makes a noise when it is moved. She likes nothing better than a toy that rattles loudly.

5. **Seat her properly.** At this age she needs you to put her in a seat so that she can reach her toys, otherwise she might not be able to position herself properly. And even if she lies in her cot, you

may find that she becomes wedged into a corner that she cannot get out of.

6. **React to her.** She is still learning about you in this first year, just as you are still learning about her. Responding to her expression, her vocalizations and her gestures lets her know that you are interested and happy. She needs this feedback to tell her that what she is doing pleases you.

ACTION PLAN FOR ENCOURAGING YOUR CHILD'S DEVELOPMENT: 12–24 MONTHS

1. **Keep her safe, but let her explore.** Your child's natural tendency at this age is to wander all over the place, whether or not she has your permission. And her limited sense of danger means that you have to watch very carefully to see that there are no hazards involved in her play.

2. **Sing to her, and tell her rhymes.** Every child loves rhymes and songs because they are very predictable, and children like predictability. The fact that she knows what is coming next in the rhyme or in the song makes it that much more enjoyable for her.

3. **Take her to the park.** No matter how many toys you have at home for her, she will still love going to the park. The wide open spaces, the other children and families who are there, and the adventure playground all combine to make this outing highly attractive.

4. **Don't do everything for her.** Of course, she is still only a young toddler but that does not mean she should be totally dependent on you for everything. She can lift a cup up to her mouth by herself, even though she might spill some. And she can put her blocks into the toy box.

5. **Take her to parent-and-toddler groups.** She needs to mix with other children in her age group. She will learn a lot from them, and she will have good fun too. If there is no local group in your area, then if possible arrange with other parents to take turns meeting up in each other's homes.

6. **Teach her to avoid household dangers.** Household accidents are so common, and the majority of them involve young children. Your toddler will not develop a good sense of danger for another couple of years, so she needs you to guide her into the path of safety.

ACTION PLAN FOR ENCOURAGING YOUR CHILD'S DEVELOPMENT: 24–36 MONTHS

1. **Don't be afraid to say 'no' to her.** The fury of your young child can be very stressful for you and her, and the prospect of it may be enough to make you give in to her demands, in order that peace and quiet can reign once more. Yet she needs you to tell her what she can and cannot do.

2. **Teach her how to calm down.** Rages at this age are fierce, and your child will probably feel drained by the power of a tantrum. So help her relax by encouraging her to sit down and play with a quiet game or toy once the main burst of temper has passed.

3. **Give her items for imaginative play.** It does not take much. A few old jumpers, a scarf, a couple of hats and maybe a few toy helmets are all that is needed for pretend play to get underway. She and her friends will make up their own scripts as they go along.

4. **Take her to playgroup.** A playgroup can provide toys, games and other activities that you will not be able to provide at home. Your child will also learn how to play with other children when she is there, and in this way she will begin to develop basic social skills such as how to share toys.

5. **Try to reason with her, where possible.** Expect her to challenge what you say, even when you do tell her why you are setting the rule. However, if you establish a pattern of explaining reasons for rules to her, then she will gradually begin to understand.

6. **Let her reason with you.** In her anger and frustration at not being able to do what she wants, she may become flustered and her speech may be unclear. Calm her down and listen to what she has to say. You do not need to agree with her, but you should at least listen.

Summary

The first 3 years of your child's life is a time when major developmental changes occur, as she grows from being a screaming baby into a thinking, caring and feeling young child. Play is very important because it is through play that your child learns about herself and about the world around her – she also expresses her feelings through play. At each age and stage during this 3-year period, you will see many examples of play, each helping your child's development and allowing her to develop skills that she will require later on when she starts infant school. Every child is capable of play. There are lots of things you can do to encourage your child's development at each age.

(II)

TIME FOR PRE-SCHOOL

2

NURSERY OR PLAYGROUP
(3 YEARS +)

Having cared for their baby at home for the first three years, many parents start to think about regularly seeking the company of other children for their child – it is difficult to provide a full range of social experiences entirely within the home itself. And that is when you may want to consider some form of external pre-school provision (e.g. nursery, playgroup, etc.) that will broaden your child's social development. In addition, this type of provision can offer your child new educational activities, new stimulation and new interests, all of which contribute to his further development. And these experiences at the pre-school stage are part of his preparation for school a year or so later.

TYPES OF PRE-SCHOOL FACILITIES

The exact pre-school facilities available for children aged 3 to 5 years vary considerably, and depend greatly on demand in your local area. However, the typical range of possibilities for this age group usually includes the following:

- **nursery schools/classes/units:** Run by the Education Department of the local authority, these are open 10 half-day sessions per week, for approximately 40 weeks in each year.

They take on average 51 children – aged 3 to 5 years – per session (though many nursery schools are smaller/larger), and staff have teaching qualifications or nursery nurse training. Demand for places in these nurseries often outstrips supply. Each local authority has clear criteria for prioritizing applications, with priority given to children from disadvantaged backgrounds. There is no charge to parents.

- **day nurseries:** Run by the Social Services Department of the local authority, these are open all day, every week of the year, and are attended by approximately 45 children per session. Children are admitted from the age of 6 months onwards; many children attend for full days. Unlike nursery classes, day nurseries are generally run by nursery nurses rather than by teachers. Hours of attendance can be flexible, to meet the needs of working parents. Demand for places in these nurseries often outstrips supply. Every establishment has a clear set of rules for allocating places, and these always give preference to children from areas of deprivation. Parents usually do not have to pay anything.

- **independent nurseries:** These are similar to the nursery schools, classes, or units operated by the local authority, except that on average they take only 28 children per session. Although these nurseries are privately run, they are supervised and licensed by the local authority and this ensures adequate standards of care and stimulation. Staffing qualifications vary greatly. Many private nurseries are more formal than would normally be expected for pre-school children, with an atmosphere more akin to the infant classroom. Costs for attendance are met in full by the parents.

- **playgroups:** These are almost entirely run by parents, under the auspices and guidance of the Pre-School Playgroup Association. They are usually based in church halls or community halls. Most of the children are under 4 years of age. Until recently playgroup staff had no professional training in early child development, but this has now changed as a result of new legislation (if you want to find out more about this, contact the Pre-school Playgroups Association at the address given in the Useful Addresses section of this book). Equipment is taken out of cupboards at the start of each day and put back again when the session is over because the hall will be used by another community group next. Parents pay a small fee for each session that their child attends.

- **childminders:** Under new regulations, all childminders must be registered with their local authority – this ensures a proper vetting system for people licensed to offer care for young children. Childminders undergo no formal training, although training opportunities are beginning to become available. A childminder will care for only a few children at any one time. The majority of parents use a childminder more to care for their child for a few hours each day (e.g. after school, before the parents return from work) than to provide stimulation.

- **nannies:** Although nannies are most commonly employed to care for children under the age of 3 years, there are many parents who value their nanny's training and expertise so much that they ask her to take responsibility for their child's care and education between the ages of 3 and 5. This can be a suitable arrangement depending on the nanny and the family's circumstances. Where a nanny is asked to take on the role of educator in the pre-school years, she should be encouraged to organize regular outings with other children so that the child meets other children his own age.

There is no guarantee that any of these options will give your child a better start to school when that moment finally arrives. However, research studies confirm that children who have some form of structured pre-school experience usually cope better with the early stages of formal schooling than those children who have not had this experience.

One survey, for instance, involved approximately 15,000 children. Their intelligence and attainments were assessed when they were 5 years old and then again when they were 10 years old, providing a unique opportunity to assess the long-term effects of pre-school provision. When the researchers compared children who had experienced nursery or playgroup with those who had not, they found that:

- children who did not attend any pre-school provision gained lower scores on tests for language developmental, intelligence, listening skills, mathematical understanding and reading ability.

- it did not really matter whether the children attended local education authority nurseries, independent nurseries or day nurseries – the benefit was seen, irrespective of the precise nature of the nursery.

But these results cannot apply for every single child. If you are able to extend your child's experiences on your own – for example, with a range of outings, access to indoor and outdoor play facilities, etc. – then he will not lose out by not attending nursery or playgroup.

CHOOSING A NURSERY/PLAYGROUP

You have to make an informed choice when you send your child to a nursery, playgroup, childminder or when you employ a nanny – you should not make your selection simply because someone told you good things about a particular group, or because it is just round the corner. Pre-school provision is an important part of your child's life, so it is worth taking some time to investigate. (In addition to the comments below, read Chapter 8, as many of the points

raised there are relevant here too). Here are some basic
principles to guide you:

- **Visit the playgroup/nursery/childminder before agreeing to send your child there.** You need to see the facilities for yourself and to talk to the staff who will be caring for your child.

- **Go with an open mind.** Try to leave aside any preconceived ideas you have about the nursery or childminder since these can cloud your perspective. Be prepared to like – or dislike – what you see.

- **Ask other parents whose child attends there.** You may find it useful to talk to other parents whose children are there – as long as you do not make their views the sole basis of your choice.

- **Study the nursery's handbook.** Each establishment catering for the needs of young children has a small handbook that outlines its aims and objectives, as well as providing factual details such as times, costs, number of staff, etc.

Ask Questions

During your visit there are a number of basic questions that need to be answered before you can make an informed choice about whether or not your child should attend there. These include:

- *How long will it take me to get there and back with my child?* This is an important factor to take into account. Bear in mind that you will have to make this journey up to 10 times each week, come rain, hail or shine! A 20-minute journey may be manageable once a week during the summer, but it may become completely impractical every day during the winter.

- *How much time will he spend there?* Nursery and playgroup hours vary. As you may be trying to dovetail your child's attendance at nursery with the hours of your own employment, timing could be a crucial factor. Some nurseries start very early in the morning and finish late in the day, providing flexible care, while others are more rigid. Sessions are often either mornings only or afternoons only.

- *What is the cost?* Local authority nurseries do not charge for the service they provide (although there may be a long waiting list), nor do day nurseries run by the local Social Services department. Private nurseries do charge a flat monthly rate for every child, irrespective of parental income, and this full rate is paid even when a child has occasional absences. Do not be afraid to ask the current costs. Playgroup charges are generally nominal.

- *Will I need to take part in a rota for supervising the children?* Unlike most playgroups, nurseries do not have a requirement that every parent becomes involved in a supervision rota. However, there will be opportunities for you to join in some of the activities in the nursery – if you can, take advantage of this.

It will please your child and allow you to experience the atmosphere of the nursery for yourself.

- *Do I like what is going on in the nursery or playgroup?* Look around the nursery, observing the children, the staff and the overall atmosphere of the facility. The activities should be varied and challenging so that the children appear interested, stimulated and motivated, and there should be plenty of examples of the children's artwork decorating the walls. Nurseries should be lively and stimulating.

- *Can the group offer my child more than I can?* One of the reasons for sending your child to nursery or playgroup is that you expect it to provide things that you are unable to at home (e.g. mixing with others, a broad range of intellectually stimulating activities, etc.). Compare the regular programme offered by the nursery or playgroup to the sort of programme that you can provide at home for your child.

- *Is there a big variety of indoor and outdoor toys?* Play is the medium through which your child learns, particularly in these pre-school years. A good playgroup or nursery should have a wide variety of different toys, including jigsaws and other puzzles, dressing-up clothes for imaginative play, paints and crayons, water and sand trays, construction toys and large outdoor play equipment to develop your child's movement and balance.

- *Does the atmosphere seem pleasant and friendly?* Every nursery and playgroup should be welcoming, both to the children who attend there and the adults who visit. Staff should respect their children and treat them seriously – it is better for them to use a positive approach (for instance, by using praise to encourage the children's good behaviour rather than reprimands to discourage inappropriate behaviour).

- *Will he know any other child there when he starts?* Starting anything new is always easier with a friend, and that applies just as much to your child as it does to any other. Look around the playgroup or nursery to see if there are any children that your child knows. Even if he only has a passing acquaintance with one or two of them, that will give him enough confidence to cope socially with this new experience.

A simple rule of thumb to follow is that you should not send your child anywhere (even for a few minutes) unless you feel totally comfortable about doing so. And you do not need to explain your reasoning to anyone – do what you feel is right for your child, for you and for the rest of your family.

SUMMARY

When your child reaches the age of 3 or 4 years, you will probably want to consider pre-school provision that takes him outside your home. There is a wide range of facilities available, including nurseries, playgroups, childminders and nannies. Before committing yourself, make a visit and gather as much information as you can about the services provided. Only you can decide if this particular establishment is right for your child.

FROM PRE-SCHOOL TO INFANT SCHOOL

3

READINESS FOR SCHOOL

The transition from pre-school provision to infant school is one of the biggest steps in your young child's life. At best, it signifies the beginning of a positive stage in her development, one which brings educational stimulation and endless opportunities for personal and intellectual growth. At worst, however, it can signify the beginning of a negative stage in her development, one which is marked by tension and insecurity, unsatisfactory relationships with other children and adults, and a lowering of self-esteem. (In many instances, the same applies when a child changes from one infant school to another – the same pressures exist and the same measures, outlined later in this chapter, are relevant).

The need for smooth continuity from pre-school to school is emphasized by most educationalists, some of whom use a gardening analogy when describing this phase in your child's life. When a seedling is transplanted from one place to another, the transplantation may stimulate the seedling's growth or may be such a shock that it stops the seedling's growth – and an efficient gardener tries to make the transplant process as smooth as possible so that the plant takes root again very quickly. In the same way, a child moving from a nursery to an infant class also needs very careful handling so that she is stimulated by the transition, but not overwhelmed or shocked by it.

Continuing this gardening analogy, some educationalists point out that children – like plants – are different individuals and react to the transition from nursery to the infant class in different and individual ways. One child who finds the experience difficult might become upset and tearful, whereas another might become withdrawn and apathetic. And although there are many children who do settle into the infant class with no obvious problems, there are many who find the transition difficult to some extent.

When you think about this transition from a child's point of view, it is not surprising there are lots of pupils who have problems starting school. There are so many changes to be made, changes which represent a departure from the pre-school world she knows. And this element of change is not just felt by a child who has spent her previous years at home; it is also felt by a child who has attended a playgroup, a nursery, or a childminder – because none of these matches the infant school environment exactly. Change is inevitable.

READINESS FOR SCHOOL

The notion of 'readiness' in childhood usually implies two principles: first, that a child has to reach a specific point in her development before she is ready to change, and secondly, that this point of readiness is reached spontaneously through the natural growth process.

For instance, Jerry is 6 months old and – like all infants his age – his coordination skills are at an early stage of development. Although he can move his legs in a controlled way, he has not reached the point where he is ready to start walking independently without support. And there is nothing Jerry's parents can do to help him reach that point. Until his neurological and muscular system has matured, his movements will remain limited. Only when Jerry arrives at that specific developmental stage sometime during the next 12 months – through the natural growth process – will he be ready to walk. Until then, Jerry's 'readiness to walk' cannot be significantly affected by the adults in his world.

There are many other examples of stages of readiness in childhood which are reached naturally without help from adults, and which cannot be accelerated even if adults do become involved (e.g. readiness to sit up independently, readiness for the appearance of the second set of teeth, readiness for puberty).

But the same does not apply to 'readiness for starting school', because although a child's readiness for starting school depends partly on her spontaneous development during the pre-school years (as indicated in the above examples) it also depends partly on the help and encouragement you have given her during the pre-school years. You can significantly improve your child's readiness for starting school by focusing on her development in general and by focusing on her strategies for coping specifically with the impact of the changes between nursery and school.

Readiness for School – General Development

There are many skills that will help your child settle into the infant classroom, so that schooling is a positive experience for her. These skills are listed in subsequent chapters. You may also find it helpful to have an overall idea of the general pattern of development expected of the typical 4- and 5-year-old child – the checklist below enables you to match your child's progress to date against the more general picture, and from this you will have a rough idea of her readiness for starting school. There are five important dimensions of your child's general development that are closely linked to her readiness for starting school.

1. **development of learning.** Your child's natural learning ability means that she can gain knowledge from her past experiences and use that to have a better understanding of future experiences. Learning skills allow her to interpret the world around her so that she can be more successful the next time. The term 'intelligence' is sometimes used instead of 'learning skills'.

2. **development of movement.** She needs a variety of skills that help her coordinate her leg movements (for example when running, hopping, walking), her arm movements (when catching, throwing, carrying) and also that help her maintain her balance (as when moving forward, turning, stopping). All these skills interact with each other.

3. **development of speech.** Your child has to understand what is said to her and also to be able to use words to say what she feels or wants. The ability to communicate with words is very important for learning; and children who have a speech

problem can have difficulties making themselves understood to other children, which causes frustration and isolation.

4. **development of self.** Mixing with others is essential at this age, as is having a good level of self-confidence. If she feels good about herself, she will enjoy nursery and school more. In addition, your child needs to be able to cope without you beside her all the time, to be able to manage on her own, for instance at mealtimes, when using the bathroom and when putting on her jacket.

5. **development of hand control.** There are many tasks and activities at this age, involving your child's ability to control her hands. For instance, she needs to hold a crayon or pencil properly when drawing, and she needs to lift a fork and spoon when eating. Hand control is very important in infant school since many of the learning sessions are 'hands-on'.

All these different areas of development are connected with each other – none of them can develop in isolation, so take a global view of your child. It is equally important not to look at her strengths and weaknesses in isolation from her background. A child at the age of 5 years may be expected to be able to cut with scissors. But if she has never had the opportunity to hold a pair of scissors ever before, then of course she will not have mastered that skill yet. Only when all the different pieces of data about your child are put together can valid conclusions be reached about her general readiness for starting school.

TYPICAL DEVELOPMENT AT 4 YEARS

Development of Learning

- Her learning skills have matured enough so that she understands the concept of comparisons, for instance, that 'big' is different from 'small', that 'fat' is different from 'slim' and so on.

- She is more interested in jigsaws and is prepared to try those that have perhaps around 15 pieces. However, once she becomes stuck and cannot quickly identify the next piece, she will give up easily.

- Early number skills develop. She may be able to count up to 10, although she will not understand the significance of each number. Place four of the same objects, for instance sweets, on a surface and ask her to count them out, pointing to each one as she does so. She may be able to do this.

- She enjoys playing with a miniature doll's house, farm set or railway station, and becomes engrossed in this.

Development of Movement

- Balance is sound. You will find that your child can undertake a variety of physical tasks successfully, such as hopping a few paces on one foot, walking steadily along a straight line or travelling up and down stairs, one foot in front of the other, without any help.

- She likes kicking a ball along the ground. She is able to connect her foot with the ball when it is static but not when it is rolling at all.

- She will happily climb on to the back of a rocking horse, seat herself securely, then start rocking backwards and forwards.

- Your child enjoys participating in catching and batting games. Her arm coordination is more advanced at this age.

Development of Speech

- Her speech is completely intelligible. She has a broad vocabulary, with an ample use of personal pronouns and adjectives.

- She can tell you about something that has just happened to her – the details may be jumbled but it will make sense.

- Nursery rhymes and songs are very popular. She does not need much prompting to join in with you.

- She loves to laugh, even though she may not fully appreciate the joke. She realizes that laughing is good fun, and that it is part of being sociable.

- By now she is aware that colours have different names, and she may know one or two of these.

Development of Hand Control

- When she draws a sketch of you, the picture now resembles a human being, and she may include minor characteristics such as eyes and ears, arms and legs.

- She enjoys bead-threading and can cope with a thinner piece of thread and smaller beads.

- She is able to cut more accurately with scissors. She may find that the paper seems very tough but she should manage to cut from one side to the other.

- Give your child some crayons and a blank sheet of paper. Ask her to draw a picture of her house. Although details will be missing, you will see that her drawing is recognizable.

- Your child is able to coordinate her finger movements in a way that allows her to pick up a very small object that is lying on the floor.

Development of Self

- She is no longer content to play on her own or just alongside children; she now takes an active role, cooperating with them. She knows that games can only succeed if everyone follows the rules, and tries hard not to get angry when she does not win.

- Your child is more independent when undressing herself. However, you are still needed for those tricky little fasteners that are too hard for young children to undo.

- She should be able to tell her age when asked by someone she knows.

- Your child takes an interest in helping around the house. She will probably want to help you, especially when it comes to setting the table for a meal. If asked, she will be able to set out cutlery in approximately the correct places.

TYPICAL DEVELOPMENT AT 5 YEARS

Development of Learning

- Counting is more established and your child can count up to six or seven items, as long as they are in front of her and she touches them one by one as she counts.

- When she wakes up the morning she knows that she has breakfast and not dinner, and that she goes to bed at the end of each day, not the beginning. In other words, she recognizes the basic time sequence of a day.

- Take a handful of coins and ask your child to name them. She may be able to identify one of them.

- Jigsaw puzzles usually do not prove much of a problem, as long as they have an interesting picture and no more than about 20 pieces.

- She can tell you that two colours are the same or different from each other. She can also tell the names of some colours, usually blue, red, yellow and green.

Development of Movement

- Her agility has vastly improved, so that she can run all over the place without tripping. She is willing to try most physical challenges.

- She makes a good attempt at catching a large ball – using her arms and hands in a large pincer-type movement – if it is thrown gently to her. She can run up to a ball and then kick it, without stopping.

- Games involving balance become part of her play activities. She will enjoy trying to master the intricacies of a skipping rope, for instance.

- Ask your child to bend and touch her toes without bending her knees. She will probably be able to do this, although she might require some practice before mastering it.

Development of Speech

- Your child enjoys discussing things with you, taking pleasure out of listening and out of talking. She probably has very firm opinions about everything and does not hesitate to express her thoughts to you.

- Her speech is easy to understand. She can say what she thinks or wants and the listener knows what she means.

- At this age it is important that she is able to say her full name and where she lives, just in case she gets lost.

- Her sentences are longer and are grammatically correct, with nouns coming before verbs and words in the right places.

Development of Hand Control

- Her use of scissors has vastly improved; she may be able to cut round a shape that is drawn on a piece of paper.

- You will find that with a bit of practice she can copy a large letter using a pencil or thin crayon. She can copy shapes too.

- She tries desperately hard to cope with small fasteners on her clothes and she may be able to succeed if she persists. However, it will be difficult for her, so it is best not to buy her, for instance, shoes with lots of fiddly little buckles.

- Your child enjoys arts and craft activities because she has a good imagination and she has sufficient hand control to cut, glue and paint.

Development of Self

- Your child sits properly at the dinner table and eats her meal independently without making a terrible mess.

- She takes more responsibility for looking after herself at home. Of course you still need to tidy up after her wherever she goes, but she does show encouraging signs of making an effort.

- She can be remarkably protective when she sees a younger child who is hurt or upset, and she will usually try to reduce other children's distress.

- Your child needs the company of other children at times because she can have great fun playing group games. However, she still enjoys playing quietly on her own.

- She goes happily to playgroup or nursery, without becoming upset when she sees you walk away from her.

READINESS FOR SCHOOL – SPECIFIC CHANGES

As well as considering these general developmental factors affecting your child's readiness for school, let us take a closer look at some of the specific changes associated with starting the infant class. Your awareness of these factors means that you can prepare your child for them:

Factor 1: The School Building

Playgroups usually function in one room, and even large nurseries occupy two or three large rooms at most – and these rooms are frequently self-contained in one small building. Toilets will be close by, and every pre-school facility will be used only by children who are relatively close to each other in age. Compare this with the infant classroom of a large primary school: even though the first class may be self-contained, it still functions as part of a larger infant section – and as part of an even larger primary school.

How to encourage readiness for the school building:

1. Give your child a chance to become familiar with her new school building, before the school term. Take her round the rooms she is likely to use – including the toilet, dining areas, and playground.

2. When visiting the school with her, make sure she is aware of the areas that are designated for infants and those that are designated for older pupils. She should see all of these areas.

3. Reassure her that she will get to know the layout of the building, even though she may be unsure of her way around at first. Remind her that all the other children starting in her class will be in the same situation.

Factor 2: The Curriculum

Tremendous strides have been made in nursery education in recent years in order to match the pre-school curriculum with that of the infant class activities, and there is clear overlap between what children learn in these two phases of their education. There are, however, many instances where this does not apply, creating the possibility of confusion in a young child's mind. And, of course, there are many under-fives who have never set foot in nursery before they start school. An unfamiliar infant curriculum can be daunting.

How to encourage readiness for the curriculum:

1. Make sure your child has some experience of the sort of classroom activities she will meet in her new school. If you are at all in doubt, talk to her teacher – she will be able to advise you on suitable tasks.

2. Give her a sample of other aspects of the curriculum which she may not have seen while in the nursery. PE, in particular, is something that many infant pupils find especially challenging because it is unfamiliar.

3. Try to become familiar with the sort of work carried out in the first infant class so that you can introduce your child to the range of materials and programme of study she is likely to meet there.

Factor 3: The Expectations

Fortunately, the distinction between caring for pre-school children and educating pre-school children has become blurred. No longer is nursery seen simply as a care facility, and no longer is school seen simply as a place where children experience formal education. However, expectations of children in school tend to be different from (and more demanding than) those in the nursery.

How to encourage readiness for expectations:

1. Encourage your child to become independent and less reliant on adults. Help her master basic tasks such as putting her coat on, dressing and undressing (e.g. for PE), and eating lunch.

2. Give her practice working in small groups with other children. This will improve her listening and social skills, her concentration, and her ability to respond to group (rather than individual) instructions.

3. Try to decrease the amount of individual attention you give her during the day, whether you are with her at home or in the nursery. She should be able to complete a basic task without seeking your help.

Factor 4: The Pupils and Teachers

Compared to nurseries, playgroups and childminders, infant schools have many more pupils and far fewer adults to look after them. Each child has more peer-group relationships to deal with than ever before. In addition, a new infant pupil moves from being the oldest child in the nursery (i.e. at the top of the 'pecking order') to the youngest child in the school (i.e. at the bottom of the 'pecking order'). And there is less individual adult attention available for children in school than there was for them at the pre-school stage.

How to encourage readiness for the pupils and teachers:

1. The more opportunities she has to mix with other children her own age – in both formal and informal settings – then the more ready she will be to mix with her classmates in school.

2. She will adapt more easily to her new teacher/teachers if she is used to meeting new adults. Therefore, in nursery, encourage her to spend some time with all the nursery nurses, if possible.

3. Explain to her in advance that although she is in the oldest group in nursery, she will be in the youngest class at school. Reassure her that she has nothing to fear from this shift in age groupings.

Factor 5: The Routine

Of course, every infant class strives to have a happy and industrious atmosphere. But routine is still an essential aspect of the infant school day, more so than in a nursery or playgroup. Routine provides a structure to the day's activities and gives children the opportunity to plan ahead. Each pupil is expected to be aware of – and to follow – the routine within her particular classroom, and within the other areas of the school. Inability to cope with this more formal routine could cause your child to have problems organizing herself and her workload.

How to encourage readiness for the routine:

1. In the few months before starting school, try to structure your child's day so that there is an element of regularity. Ask her to predict some of the activities later that morning or afternoon.

2. Give her practice in planning for anticipated activities. For example, if she knows you are taking her swimming, ask her to prepare her swimming gear well in advance of your expected leaving time.

3. Let your child devise some of her own routines at home, even at a basic level. She is more likely to feel comfortable about following a routine that takes her own views into account.

Summary

The transition between pre-school life and school life is a major stage in your young child's life, and the more 'ready' she is for school the better. But her readiness depends on the help and stimulation you provide for her at home. There are many general skills expected of a typical 4- or 5-year-old so that schooling becomes a positive experience.

In addition to your child's general development, there are several specific factors that affect her readiness for school, including the school building, the curriculum, the expectations, the pupils and teachers, and the school routine – and you can help your child prepare for these.

THRIVING IN INFANT SCHOOL

PERSONALITY COUNTS

Ask any infant teacher to list the characteristics of pupils who are most likely to thrive in an infant class: although she is likely to mention educational features such as 'intelligence', 'competence' and 'good use of language', the chances are that these will not be top of the list—instead, personality traits are more likely to be in first place, especially during the first year at infant school.

That doesn't mean that a child's intellectual ability isn't important for achievement in school, just that settling in to the infant class can depend more on a child's emotional characteristics. The chart below lists the main personality features that matter, and explains why they are so important.

Characteristic	Significance
Positive attitude	Your child needs a positive approach to learning, so that he is enthusiastic and tries hard at all the activities he becomes involved with. Without this outlook he will not make full use of his abilities.
Self-confidence	The infant class is full of new challenges, not just on the first day, and the more confident your child is about his own strengths the

more able he will be to cope with unfamiliar activities.

Good listening skills	Most information in the infant class will be conveyed to your child verbally by his class teacher—and he needs to be good at listening or he will miss much of what goes on in the classroom, and even in small-group discussions.
Inquisitiveness	Curiosity—the desire to understand something—should be one of the main driving forces behind a child's learning. Your child's willingness to ask questions of his teacher will increase his learning.
Respect for others	Cooperation between pupils is an essential ingredient of a happy classroom atmosphere, and this starts in the infant class. Your child's awareness of others' feelings, and his respect for them, is important.
Low aggression	Every day at infant school—in the classroom, in the corridor and in the playground—there are moments of conflict, and your child should be able to resolve these without becoming aggressive.

PLAY YOUR PART

These personality features do not develop spontaneously. It is not a matter of luck that one child arrives in the infant class bursting with enthusiasm while another arrives in the same class lacking any interest whatsoever; or that one child is self-confident and thirsty for knowledge while another feels insecure and does not ask questions. Much depends on the child's pre-school experiences.

Rachel is in her last year at nursery and is due to start school in the next few months. Both her parents work and she has an older brother who will be four years ahead of her at the same school. Rachel's parents did not like school when they were pupils, but they recognize how much things have changed since then.

Quite simply, they marvel at the broad range of the curriculum and the new computer technology that they see their son using in class. It is not surprising that Rachel is already enthusiastic about this next stage in her young life.

Next door to Rachel, Joe lives with his parents, who both work full-time. He also has two older sisters. Neither sister gets on well in school and Joe's parents have had to make frequent visits to speak to the class teachers about their daughters' behaviour. As a result, the adults and children in Joe's house view school negatively, regarding it as an establishment that is more concerned with discipline than with learning. Joe does not attend nursery because his parents do not think pre-school provision is worth while. It is not surprising that Joe has a negative outlook on school, even though he has not started there yet.

1. How to Develop your Child's Positive Attitude

Of course, a child's ability has an influence on his success at school. But his attitude towards learning and towards school in general will determine whether or not he uses that ability. A positive attitude shows through in many ways, including a general enthusiasm for educational activities within the infant classroom, a desire to please the class teacher, a willingness to try hard at every assignment presented to him, and a desire to tell you all about his experiences when you collect him at the end of the school day. You can greatly influence your child's attitude towards school, both before he starts his day there and after it.

Here are ways to encourage your child's enthusiasm for the infant class:

- *Whenever you speak about school in front of your child, talk enthusiastically about it. Your obvious zeal will rub off on him and he will eventually feel the same way that you do.*

- *Mention specific features about the infant school that you know he will like, such as the availability of computers, the wider range of equipment, the play activities during intervals, etc.*

- *Tell him about some of the things you enjoyed at school (even if it was not a particularly happy time for you). Although school has changed since you attended, your memories will interest him.*

- *Never use school as a threat to your child, or suggest that the teachers there are extremely strict. This will only make him afraid, rather than encourage him to look forward to starting school.*

- *Suggest to him that he plays at 'schools' with his friends every so often. This imaginative play activity will help release any fears or negative feelings he might have about the prospect of attending school.*

- *When taking your child on a pre-admission visit to his future school, let him have a look at the actual classroom he will use. Point out how attractive it is, the wide range of books, etc.*

- *Have a quiet word with his brothers and sisters, if possible, to make sure that they do not overwhelm him with the sorts of horror stories about school that older siblings love to tell their little brother and sisters.*

- *Take him with you when you purchase school-related equipment such as his bag, shoes, jumper, etc. Let him be involved in choosing the purchases, although the final decision will obviously rest with you.*

- *Encourage him to voice his feelings about the prospect of attending school. If he mentions specific anxieties, reassure him that he has nothing to worry about.*

- *Take an interest in his school day. Some children are not very communicative about what has happened in school that day, but ask him anyway since that shows you are interested.*

2. How to Develop your Child's Self-confidence

A child who has a low level of self-confidence will have an uphill struggle settling into the infant class. Psychological research confirms that children who are lacking in self-confidence tend to do less well at school than would be expected on the basis of their intellectual ability, and have greater difficulty making new friends with other children in their class.

Here are ways to boost your child's self-confidence for starting school:

- *Give him the opportunity to experience some of the educational activities he is likely to meet in the infant class – and make them easy enough so that he is more likely to succeed than to fail.*

- *Reassure him that he is capable and competent enough to do well at school. Point out his strengths (e.g. that he knows colours, shapes, etc.), and explain that this means he will cope with anything he is asked to do.*

- *If he does have anxieties about starting school, listen to them – but offer practical solutions. For instance, fears about being last in the queue for school lunches can be solved by giving him a packed lunch.*

- *Have realistic expectations of your child's ability and potential achievements. Of course, you have to encourage him to reach his full potential, but do not make your expectations too high.*

- *Even if he does not have a good start to the infant class, do not show your concern. Talk to him calmly; try to identify the areas that are causing him difficulty and offer suggestions for improvement.*

- *Do not let him become concerned with the things he is not good at. If he has too many doubts about his own ability, he may not try hard to achieve at school.*

- *When he does compare himself to the other children in his class – and it is only natural that he will do this – make sure he looks at a broad range of features, including personal as well as academic traits.*

- *If your child misbehaves in the infant class, do not repeatedly tell him how naughty he is. Constant reminders of his negative behaviour will reduce his self-respect; praise for good behaviour is more effective.*

- *Listen to your child when he wants to talk to you about something that is worrying him. Although you may not be able to offer an instant solution, he will feel better for your undivided attention.*

- *Point out to him that he thoroughly enjoyed nursery (or play-group), and that he mixed well with the other children. Tell him that the same will happen when he starts the infant class.*

3. How to Develop your Child's Listening Skills

Listening is a fundamental part of learning, but is not something that comes naturally to all children. An infant classroom has a lively atmosphere, as the young pupils begin the formal learning process. There is so much that they have to listen to, including instructions from the teacher and from each other, new information that has to be absorbed, and ideas and feelings expressed by others.

Here are ways to encourage your child's listening skills during the pre-school years:

- *When your child plays with a group of his friends, ask him to stop for a few minutes, close his eyes and try to identify whose voice it is that he hears.*

- *Suggest to him that he looks at you directly when you ask him a question or give him a brief instruction; making eye-contact like that will result in more accurate listening.*

- *Clap out a simple rhythm (e.g. two fast beats, a slow beat, and a fast beat) and ask your child to repeat this. Gradually make the rhythm more complicated, each time asking him to repeat it accurately.*

- Read short stories to him – in a room that is free from distractions – and suggest that he look at the pages while listening. Ask him simple questions about the story when you have finished.

- Make up a cassette of everyday household sounds, such as a running tap, a flushing toilet, a door closing, etc. See how many of these sounds your child can identify correctly.

- Give him a short instruction containing only one item of information (e.g. 'Bring me the cup'). Gradually extend the content of the instructions (e.g. 'Go into the kitchen and bring me a wrapped biscuit').

- Sit with your child while he is watching a children's television programme. After it has finished, ask him to tell you what happened to the main character in the programme.

- Play 'Simon says', starting off with an easy command (e.g. 'Simon says put your hand on your head') then becoming more difficult (e.g. 'Simon says put your hand on your tummy and jump up and down').

- Say two words and ask your child to say whether they are the same or not the same (e.g. table – table). At times, make the words different in various ways (e.g. table – cable, table – tumble, table – tablet).

- Place some small objects, such as buttons or dried peas, into a container, put the lid on and then shake it loudly. Ask your child to describe the sound, and to suggest what might be inside the container.

4. How to Develop your Child's Inquisitiveness

Curiosity is one of the main driving forces behind your child's desire to learn in school. Of course, there are other factors such as his need to please the teacher, his need to be accepted by his classmates, and so on – but his need to acquire knowledge constantly pushes him into finding out things he did not know before. An inquiring mind is an essential tool for a child in the infant classroom, and the ability to ask suitable questions is a good way of learning. However, he will not be prepared to ask his teacher questions unless he is confident and self-assured.

Here are ways to encourage your child's healthy inquisitiveness in the infant class:

- *Always treat his questions seriously, even though they may seem rather odd to you. If he is sufficiently interested to ask a question, then he deserves a straightforward reply.*

- *When asked a question that you do not have an answer for, tell your child. Be honest with him and show him how he can find the answer in a suitable reference book. That can be a fun activity, which is shared.*

- *Answer your child's questions in a way that he will understand, without giving too much information or too much detail. At this age he wants a quick reply, not everything you know about the topic.*

- *Explain to him that in school he will have to take turns to ask a question, that he should not shout out. Learning this social skill will avoid unnecessary confrontations with his teacher.*

- *Encourage him to ask his infant teacher questions if he is not sure about something. He should not pretend to understand when in fact he does not – that will only cause difficulties in the long run.*

- *Advise your child that he can ask questions in front of the whole class, but that some questions may be more suited to a one-to-one situation with the teacher (e.g. 'Can I sit with a different pupil?').*

- *Suggest to him that he should always make an effort to try to find an answer to his questions himself, if possible; he should only ask the teacher if he cannot resolve the matter on his own.*

- *Once your child has received a satisfactory answer, ask him to explain it to you. This is one of the best ways to verify whether or not he really understands what he has been told.*

- *Tell your child that there are reference books with lots of information, and that these provide answers to many of his questions. Show him by example, adding that he will be able to use these books himself once he can read.*

- *If he constantly pesters you with questions, avoid telling him to be quiet. A better strategy is to allow him to ask only one or two questions each time, and let him choose the ones to ask.*

5. HOW TO DEVELOP YOUR CHILD'S RESPECT FOR OTHERS

So much of the learning process in the infant class involves children working together, usually in small groups. That means your child not only has to be able to cooperate with his classmates – he also has to respect them, and to be prepared to listen to different perspectives even if these clash with his own. As parents we spend a great deal of time discouraging anti-social behaviour in our pre-school children; we should also spend time encouraging our children to be kind, considerate and caring. The atmosphere in any infant class is determined by the attitudes of the pupils towards each other, and a considerate child will find the infant class much more enjoyable.

Here are ways to encourage your child's respect for others:

- *Let your child know that what he does affects others. He may not realize that the simple act of picking up a fallen pencil and handing it to his classmate means a lot to her. Make it clear to him.*

- *Let him know how pleased you are when he acts kindly towards others. Your approval of these actions will reinforce this behaviour, and makes him realize that you value what he has done.*

- *If he asks for one, give him the present of a pet. Young children love having a goldfish or a hamster, and looking after it does not take much time or organization. This teaches them the concept of responsibility for others.*

- *Suggest that he does more to help at home. He may not like having to put an empty box into the dustbin, but through basic tasks like this he will gradually become more helpful around the house.*

- *Ask your child if he can think of any examples of his kindness towards someone else that day. Even though he might make up an instance just to please you, your question still focuses his thoughts on caring for others.*

- *Think about your own behaviour. You have to provide a suitable standard for your child to copy – if he sees you being horrible towards someone then he is hardly likely to behave kindly when it is his turn.*

- *When he has been in discussion with a friend, ask him to tell you what his friend said. That forces your child to give at least some thought to his friend's perspective on the matter.*

- *Practise cooperation at home. Join in with your child in activities that you can work on together (e.g. completing a jigsaw, building an object with his construction bricks), showing him how to work well with others.*

- *When you are faced with a simple practical problem (e.g. you are struggling to put away the weekly shopping), ask your child to suggest how he might help you.*

- *Make sure that he plays with toys and games that involve sharing and cooperation. Respect for others developed through play will transfer to other areas of your child's life.*

6. How to Develop your Child's Ability to Handle Aggression

There will be times when your child is aggressive, whether it is physically (by hitting, kicking or biting) or verbally (by screaming, swearing or insulting). That sort of behaviour – even though it is often shocking – is normal in childhood. All children get angry now and then, and aggression and anger are two emotions that are closely intertwined. But this behaviour is not acceptable in a school, no matter how young the pupil is, and will always be frowned upon by your child's teacher. So the more you can discourage your

child's willingness to react aggressively during the pre-school years, then the more likely he is to settle in to the infant class.

Here are ways to develop your child's ability to handle his aggression:

- *Do not smack your child when you see him fighting with one of his friends – if you use aggression to get your own way, you can hardly be surprised when your child does the same thing.*

- *Have a structured discipline at home, one that is neither too strict nor too permissive. Research shows that a child raised in a family without structured discipline is more likely to lash out in temper.*

- *Recognize the difference between aggressive behaviour and aggressive feelings. It is perfectly normal for your child to feel angry and to want to hit out in temper, but do discourage aggressive behaviour.*

- *Teach your child socially acceptable ways of releasing his aggression, such as painting, clay modelling or any form of physical exercise, including running.*

- *Explain to him about the practical effects of his aggression. Even a pre-schooler is old enough to understand when you say 'If you hit your friend, then he will not invite you to his birthday party.'*

- *Discourage your child from playing only with toy guns, toy weapons and toy soldiers. There is evidence that regularly playing with this type of toy can increase your child's aggression.*

- *When your child watches a violent television programme, explain to him that it is not real, and that he should not imitate what he sees on television because it is only make-believe.*

- *Soothe his anger with calmness, not with anger of your own. If your child is agitated, hold him gently in your arms, calm him down, and ask him to tell you what is troubling him.*

- *If you and your partner disagree over ways of handling your child's difficult behaviour, try to reach a compromise agreement through joint discussion – it is in your child's and your own best interests.*

- *React appropriately when your child swears. Do not be too extreme or he will learn that swearing is a good way of agitating you. Instead, quietly reprimand him.*

Summary

Although your child's long-term success in school will depend partly on his ability and educational achievements, personality factors also play a significant role, especially in the first infant class. Many teachers confirm that the most important characteristics enabling a child to make a good start to school include having a positive attitude, strong self-confidence, a willingness to listen, respect and consideration for others, and control over aggression. There is lots you can do during your child's pre-school years in order to encourage these personality traits – if you do, then it will be time well spent.

5

ENCOURAGING YOUR CHILD'S INDEPENDENCE

What is the adult:child ratio in your child's nursery? Is it 1:14, 1:12 or maybe even 1:8? When you consider that the teacher:child ratio in the first infant class can be up to 1:30 or higher, it's not surprising that your child needs to be more independent when starting school than she was in the nursery! There is simply less adult attention to go round, and pupils are expected to do more for themselves.

Although you might be worried at the prospect of your child having to cope in the more demanding environment of the primary school, at least you can be reassured there is lots you can do to improve her independence skills so that she takes the start to primary school in her stride.

INDEPENDENCE GOALS

The chart below lists 10 'independence goals' that many infant teachers expect pupils to have attained by the time they reach school-age—and you can practise these with your child in the year prior to her joining the infant class:

Independence Skill	Further Explanation
Manages her coat	She may not have the hand-eye coordination to deal with small fastenings, but she should be able to put her arms through the sleeves and then pull her jacket or coat round her shoulders. Having removed her coat, she should hang it on her peg in the cloakroom.
Copes with the toilet	Your child should know to go to the toilet without being told, and to be able to dress herself after using it. She should also know how to wash and dry her hands before leaving the toilet area.
Separates well	If she already attends nursery, then she will have learned to cope with this before starting school, but if she hasn't had that experience then she may find the daily separation from you difficult, especially in the early weeks.
Follows instructions	In the infant class, instructions will be directed more at groups of children and less at individuals (e.g. 'All the children in the red group, get out their reading books'). Your child should be able to listen and respond to these general commands.
Takes off shoes	Most parents send infant children to school in shoes that have easy fastenings (e.g. velcro) rather than footwear with shoelaces or buckles. Whatever her shoes' fastenings, however, she should be able to close them without help.
Moves around school well	Although a substantial part of your child's school day will be spent in her classroom, she will still have to find her way from the class to the toilet area, to the dining area

and to the playground area. She should find these major areas on her own.

Completes task/activity	Young children like adult attention and it's only natural that your child will ask for help from her teacher. However, she will be expected at least to make an effort at completing a piece of work before approaching her teacher for the solution.
Eats lunch	Lunchtime is an important part of your child's school day, yet it is a time when there is less supervision. Even infant pupils are expected to be able to sit at the lunch table, to eat their meal tidily without making a mess, and to tidy the table when finished.
Gives clear answers	Your child will be asked lots of questions posed to her by her teacher, and you should encourage her to give answers that go beyond 'yes' and 'no'. And suggest to her that she make direct eye-contact with the adult who is talking to her.
Concentrates	Most of the learning tasks that your child has to deal with in the first class are short, but each learning activity requires her concentration so that she completes it within a reasonable time limit. She should be able to ignore distractions.

These are the main items of independence that will help your child when she starts school, but this list is not exhaustive. Perhaps you can think of others. Imagine your child's daily school routine, from the moment she leaves the house in the morning until the moment she returns at the end of the day. Jot down all the things she has to do independently—you may be astonished at the length of your list.

PARENTAL ATTITUDES

How much importance do you attach to your child's independence? Psychologists have divided parental attitudes towards independence into three categories:

1 autocratic: This type of parent is described as one who gives the child no freedom to express her own ideas and feelings, who always makes decisions for the child, and who does not offer the child any explanation for household rules.

2 democratic: This type of parent is described as one who allows the child to participate in family decision-making by letting her make many small decisions on her own, though at the same time retaining the final say in what the child can and cannot do.

3 permissive: This type of parent is described as one who gives the child total freedom to do as she pleases, encouraging her to do what she wants irrespective of the wishes of others, and who takes no part in placing limits on the child's behaviour.

Research studies comparing these three different styles of parental behaviour and their respective impact on the child's dependence have found, not surprisingly, that the child of democratic parents tends to be more independent than the child of either permissive parents or of autocratic parents. And the more that parents offer their child explanations for rules of behaviour, then the greater is the child's level of independence.

Democratic parenting – coupled with regular explanations of why certain rules are adhered to in the family – encourages independence for several reasons. First, the child is provided with many supervised opportunities for testing out her own ideas. This gives her a chance to think independently, while at the same time to be protected from any inappropriate decisions she might make. Secondly, the child's confidence is increased because she feels loved and respected, instead of feeling either controlled or uncared for. Thirdly, democratic parents themselves are usually independent-minded and so the child models herself on their own attitudes.

10-POINT ACTION PLAN FOR IMPROVING YOUR CHILD'S INDEPENDENCE

Encouraging your child to be independent along the lines required for starting school can be tiresome because of the demands it makes on you. But do not simply hope for the best. You need a structured plan, along the following lines, so that you and your child will be able to move together towards establishing independence:

1. **Identify the goal you would like your child to reach.** Your child should be given a clear target to aim for. For instance, 'washing your hands after you have been to the toilet', 'drinking your milk without spilling any of it' or 'asking the teacher for help when you do not know what to do'. This sort of target – clear and precise – ensures that your child knows what to do.

2. **Explain the goals to your child.** There should not be any secret about what you are doing – let your child know what the target is. Tell her exactly what you expect of her, so that she is not in any doubt. She will be pleased that you are taking an interest, and that in itself acts as a further incentive to fulfil your expectations.

3. **Improve your child's independence in gradual stages.** If she thinks that you are asking too much of her all at once, she will give up very early on. However, if she thinks the target is reasonable and attainable, then she will try hard to reach it. For instance, if she cannot unbutton her coat, the first step might be for her to undo only one of the buttons.

4. **Move on to the next stage only when the previous stage has been mastered.** There is no point in progressing until your child feels confident about her current achievements. However, once she is competent at a particular stage, do not be afraid to move her on so that she builds on her successes. She will respond to your guidance.

5. **Reinforce her success with praise.** There is every likelihood that your child finds the whole process of becoming independent quite challenging, perhaps even provoking her anxiety. She needs your reassurance that her efforts will pay off eventually – a word of encouragement, an approving smile when she succeeds, is all that is required.

6. **Have realistic expectations of your child.** You may feel social pressures to push your child to achieve at a level normally only reached by a child who is much older. But remember that all children are different; not every child starting infant school will have attained the skills listed earlier. Your child is a unique individual.

7. **Give her time.** Coping with new challenges takes time. Your child needs to feel relaxed and confident or else she will not achieve. There is no point in hurrying her along too quickly, or her desire to persist will evaporate. Allow her time to do what is required, although there is no harm in reminding her to speed up a little if you think she is not really trying.

8. **Be relaxed and supportive, not stressed.** Of course you want your child to be as independent as possible, because you are aware of the problems facing her if she is not sufficiently self-reliant. But try to avoid conveying this concern to your child, or she will simply become anxious about it herself – and this will have the effect of slowing her progress.

9. **Explain to your child why you are doing this.** She may see no advantage in being able to do things for herself, and may be content with the status quo. Explain to her why she should be independent – for instance because she will have more fun in school if she does not have to wait for someone else to help her.

10. **Give her plenty of practice at home.** Some of the goals for independence (such as finding her way round the school building) are related directly to the school context, but they should still be practised at home where possible. The boost to her self-confidence when she becomes more independent at home will carry over to school.

SOCIAL INDEPENDENCE

The ability to be independent socially, to mix well with other children and to work together with peers in a small group within the classroom, is also essential for a good start to the primary school. A child who lacks this form of social independence will have difficulties meeting the demands of the infant class.

Psychologists have identified a number of key social skills that help children settle into a new school, and these can be developed in the pre-school years. Of course, having these skills is no guarantee that your child will cope socially, but they go a long way towards it. The main ones are discussed below.

Your child's should be able to *communicate effectively*. Misunderstandings with classmates often stem from a child's inability to communicate her emotions and desires through spoken language. If your child learns to express her feelings by making the statement 'I would like to sit on that chair because my books are on that desk,' she is less likely to be rejected than if she simply goes up and pushes the other child off the chair without saying a word. You can enhance your child's communication skills by encouraging her to voice her feelings, instead of acting them out impulsively. When suitable opportunities arise during the day while with you at home, ask her questions about how she is feeling, and what she is thinking. That gets her into the habit of using words, rather than actions, to communicate.

As you have probably found from your own experiences of meeting new people, the first few moments in any social encounter are often the most difficult. If your child is *socially confident* enough to cope with these opening moments then she is likely to get on better with others. Teach her what to do when she meets a child whom she does not know. For example, she can ask him his name, or what he likes best about nursery. Practise these techniques in role-play situations at home.

At some point during play, your child will be asked by her friend to *share* her toys, and her unwillingness to do this will cause her to find play situations stressful. (Only children often find sharing especially difficult because they are so used to having everything for themselves.) Teach your child how to share, using two methods. First, explain to her why she should share. Use reasons that are meaningful to her, for instance, that sharing gives everyone a turn, that other children will like her if she shares her toys, and so on. Secondly, teach sharing by example. When you see your child arguing with her friend over a game, you may be tempted to separate the children and to remove the game altogether as a punishment. However, this will only teach her to fight quietly, without attracting your attention. Far better to show your child how to play without fighting. And once she is able to share, she will be more relaxed in the company of other children because she will not worry all the time about hanging on doggedly to her possessions.

Social independence also involves the acceptance of *turn-taking* – your child cannot possibly play games or work successfully in a small group with other children without being able to take turns. But a young child is only concerned with herself, and the ability to wait while others receive attention first does not come naturally, it has to be learned. There are many opportunities at home for teaching this social skill to your child, before she arrives in the infant classroom. Waiting her turn to tell her father some piece of news, or waiting till her brother gets a cup of juice before she does, allows your child to experience turn-taking under your supervision. Eventually she will begin to accept turn-taking as a normal part of social interactions.

Your child cannot join in games with her friends unless she is able to *follow the rules*. The social skill of following rules is fundamental to any situation that involves more than one person interacting with others. As with all social skills, however, this can be taught at home. Play games that involve rules with your child. Explain to her why games have rules and why they should be followed. If she learns this through playing with you, then the chances are she will be able to apply this to playing games with her friends.

Close investigation of play patterns among children under the age of 5 years has revealed that a child who gives *positive reinforcement* (i.e. a minor reward for good behaviour) to other children will have a higher level of social acceptance. So encourage your child to show approval of her friends and to praise them when they do things that she likes. These simple strategies will enhance her ability to mix independently with others.

Another factor which will help you child to mix more easily with other pupils is a good standard of *personal hygiene*. Children can be very rejecting of someone they regard as dirty and smelly, even if the rejected child does not realize what the problem is. This will happen even in the infant class. Your child needs to be shown basic standards of health care, such as caring for her clothes, brushing her hair, washing her hands after going to the toilet, brushing her teeth in the morning and at night, and so on. Like most children she will perhaps take the easy way out in matters of hygiene if left to her own devices, so you have to encourage her to take an interest in her appearance. Looking presentable goes a long way towards being socially acceptable.

Acceptable behaviour at mealtimes has the same effect – young children are as keen as adults to have a pleasant meal. Nobody, young or old, likes to sit opposite someone who slurps, burps and dribbles her way through a meal. Lunchtime is a major part of the infant school day, and acceptable table manners are part of your child's social independence. These must be established at home during the pre-school years. Think about your own behaviour. It is not fair for you to expect your child to use cutlery properly if she does not see you doing so regularly. She will imitate the standards you set. Remember to explain to your child why good eating habits matter. A 5-year-old will not make much sense of a vague injunction such as 'It is not nice to mess your food around' because she does not agree – she thinks it is positively wonderful to spill the food over the side of her plate. She will, however, understand when you say to her 'Other children will not want to sit beside you in the lunch hall if you behave like that.'

Avoiding Conflict

Social independence also involves your child's ability to manage her aggressive feelings (and aggression from other children) without resorting to violence. Minor fights between children are a normal part of everyday life, and are inevitable. Fights at school usually start because a child:

- feels her authority is threatened by another child in her class, and so she fights her to show she is in charge

- has become extremely confident and wants to show she is more capable than any other pupil

- is very competitive and wants to win at all costs

- is encouraged by her parents to stand up for herself when compromised by other children

- is in a bad mood and releases her anger by picking on an inno-cent bystander

- has her toys or possessions taken away by another child with-out any explanation.

The reality of childhood arguments in school is that the strongest fighter most often gets her own way. And you will have a hard time convincing your child she should not fight when she sees other children use that technique effectively.

Assuming you do not approve of aggressive anti-social behaviour, you have to teach your child other ways of cop-ing with conflict – ways that do not involve physical or ver-bal assault on other children. The chart below lists some suggestions for this.

Strategy	Explanation
Negotiation	Countries settle wars through the power of negotiation, so there is no reason why a minor skirmish in the classroom or playground cannot be sorted out in the same way. Negotiation involves your child stating her position, then letting the other child have his say. Then the two children have to agree what course of action to take. You may be surprised to see how effectively children are able to use this technique.
Talking	By the time your child has reached school age, she should be able to say what troubles her. And that is a far better strategy than giving vent to her feelings physically. Other children will be prepared to listen to her, as long as she is reasonable, and they will be reasonable towards her. Explain to her that disagreements are never properly resolved by the use of hands–talking always leads to a more long-term solution.

Change   In the same way that you might go for a short walk when you are in a bad mood in order to make you feel better, your child's anger can ease through a change in her situation. For instance, if she is arguing with another child she could, for example, walk away or suggest that they move into the classroom. A simple change of environment is often sufficient to cool down the tempers of two children who are embarked on a course of conflict.

Conciliation   A child who is being aggressive and is ready to fight shows this in her behaviour, even if she does not say a word. Her body muscles will be tense, her hands will be made into fists and her face will carry an angry expression. However, a non-aggressive child has a more conciliatory stance, looks relaxed and has a friendly look on her face—and having this outward appearance makes conflict less likely. Encourage your child to adopt these habits in school.

SUMMARY

The number of children in your child's infant class means that she is expected to be reasonably independent, to be able to look after herself without relying too much on her teacher's attention. There are a number of basic skills that teachers often expect a child to have attained by the time she reaches school age (e.g. listens to instructions, manages at the toilet without help, moves around the school by herself, etc.), and you can teach her these informally at home. You should have a clear plan of action for helping your child achieve independence.

Social independence is also important for school. There are social skills that you can help your child acquire in the pre-school years. The ability to avoid conflict with other children is another aspect of independence that will enable your child to settle into school comfortably.

6

LEARNING IN THE CLASSROOM

Once your child has settled into his new infant class and feels more comfortable in these novel surroundings, the serious business of learning gets underway. It is at this point that his thinking skills come into play, because success in school also depends on your child's ability to progress through the curriculum at a satisfactory rate. (Psychologists use several different terms to refer to thinking skills – these include 'intelligence', 'cognitive ability' and 'learning skills', all of which are used synonymously.)

Right from birth your child has thinking skills, and these continue to develop naturally throughout his pre-school years and beyond. Thinking skills enable your child to make sense of what is going on around him, to learn from his past experience, to adapt to changing circumstances, to see relationships between events and to consider abstract concepts and problems. Your child's thinking skills affect the rate at which he learns to read, write, spell and count.

This does not mean that your child has to be clever in order to cope with the new educational activities of the infant school. What it does mean, however, is that a child who has the thinking skills normally expected of a 5-year-old will find starting school that much easier. So it is worth preparing him as best you can at home.

THE ORIGINS OF THINKING SKILLS

Nobody knows for certain where your child's thinking skills come from. Some say that intelligence is inherited, just like many other personal characteristics; others say that intelligence is acquired from experience as your child develops. Let us look at each perspective in turn.

You probably see a strong physical resemblance between you and your child, and the chances are that other people have said 'He's so like you.' This similarity in appearance does not occur by chance; it happens because physical characteristics are directly inherited from the parents, through the genes. Theorists who support the heredity viewpoint suggest that if these qualities are passed from parent to child, then surely other qualities such as intelligence are also passed from generation to generation in the same way. Indeed, you may notice that your child learns in the same way that you do (that is, he needs lots of repetition before understanding things, just like you, or he finds arithmetic difficult, just like you).

Yet theorists who maintain that experience plays a vital role in development claim that intelligence is acquired, that your child's level of ability depends on the learning experiences and stimulation he receives during the pre-school years. After all, most parents would agree that their child's behaviour is influenced by what goes on at home (for example, aggressive parents frequently have aggressive children), so surely other aspects of their child (such as his intelligence) are also affected the same way. Some psychologists claim a child's level of intelligence can significantly improve if he is taught *how* to think – researchers have found experimental evidence to support this notion.

There is probably some truth in both views: your child's

intelligence derives partly from his innate ability and partly from the experiences and stimulation you provide for him at home. Accept your child's thinking skills for what they are, but help him to extend them further where possible.

CHECKLIST

Here is a brief checklist of the main things your child will probably be expected already to have learned by the time he sets foot in the infant class. (Of course, they are not essential – but they do make the educational demands of the first class easier to cope with). Your child should be able to:

- complete a two-part request (e.g. 'Please go over to the table in the corner and bring me a yellow brick')

- remember accurately something that he has been told (e.g. 'You have to bring an empty box to school tomorrow')

- state his first name, his last name and possibly his address as well, when asked by his teacher

- give a sensible and relevant reply to any reasonable question that is put to him directly in school

- recite numbers accurately up to 15, and identify all the numbers from 1 to 9. He may be able to count objects accurately, up to 5.

- have a good idea of the different time phases of the day, such as knowing that breakfast comes before lunch, etc.

- be able to complete jigsaws of at least 20 or 30 pieces without needing much help from an adult or from another child

- match two items that are the same colour, and be able to name at least three of the primary colours (e.g. red, blue and yellow)

- match two items that are the same basic shape, and be able to name at least three of them (e.g. circle, triangle, square)

- know several nursery rhymes (or children's songs) by heart, and be able to recite them out loud when asked

- name at least two or three coins accurately, even though he is not expected to have a clear understanding of their value

- draw a recognizable house, with windows and a door in it, and also a recognizable person with arms, legs and hands

- write one or two letters in a legible format (usually the initial letters of his first name)

- relate his recent experiences clearly to an adult, so that the listener understands what actually happened

HELPING YOUR CHILD LEARN

Here are some general points to bear in mind when trying to help your child learn at home or school:

- **Treat play seriously.** Always remember that play is the principal medium through which your child learns naturally, under the age of 5 years. He should be allowed to play with all different kinds of toys and games.

- **Speak to him.** His learning skills also develop through normal discussion with you and other children. Through the use of language he learns how to express his feelings and ideas, and how to communicate these effectively.

- **Use natural situations.** Your child uses thinking skills throughout his normal day – he uses memory to find his crayons. Experiences that arise naturally provide the best opportunities for improving learning skills.

- **Make learning fun.** Avoid the temptation to set up a formal training programme for improving your child's learning skills – he is likely to switch off and learn nothing. Far better to keep learning activities relaxed, enjoyable and fun.

- **Do not make comparisons.** It really does not matter that your friend's child seems more able than your own. Every child is different, with different strengths and weakness. Comparisons will only make you – and your child – unhappy. It is better to accept his individuality.

- **Give him practice.** Most children need to practise an activity several times before they learn how to do it properly. Encourage your child to play the same game a few times, or to read the same book again and again.

- **Praise his achievements.** When he manages to learn something new, give him lots of attention and encouragement. Your interest and praise will act as very strong incentives for him to continue developing his skills.

Your child's learning skills become extended and challenged when he starts school, as he begins to learn the wide range of subjects in the curriculum. The class teacher will advise you about the type of home-based activities to help your child's development. But whatever you do to help your child learn, remember that an anxious child often becomes so worried about the possibility of failure that he cannot concentrate while trying to learn – do not put him under unnecessary pressure.

You will also find that your child learns new concepts

more easily when he is given lots of repetition. He learns something new each time, even though he has completed the activity before. Repetition allows him to test out what he already knows, and to fill in the gaps where he is uncertain. This also builds up his confidence in his own learning abilities.

And lastly, if your child is struggling to learn something new at school, be prepared to show him how it can be done. This is not cheating. It is usually true that a child who makes a spontaneous discovery of a solution is usually more delighted than if someone tells him the answer, yet there is a place for modelling the correct example so that your child can copy you – this is another way of developing his learning. Do not do this, however, until you feel confident that he has made a genuine effort to succeed on his own.

CONCENTRATION

A child who cannot concentrate will not be able to progress much in the infant class. It does not matter how much your child enjoys the activities or how clever he is – he must be able to concentrate in order to learn. The list below outlines the key dimensions of concentration and suggests ways of improving your child's attention span. Try them with your child.

Dimension 1: Deliberately Focusing on a Specific Item

Your child should make a conscious effort to attend to what is going on around him in the classroom. This means he has to concentrate specifically on the what the teacher says, rather than just to let his concentration wander passively all over the place.

How to Help your Child Improve this Skill: When out shopping in the supermarket with your child, ask him to find one item in particular (e.g. a bag of flour). Encourage him to walk up and down the different aisles until he is able to locate it, and remind him only to look for that item.

Dimension 2: Considering Information Methodically

In class, your child will be presented with new information every day. He needs to develop his concentration so that he can sift through this information methodically in order to identify the most important elements.

How to Help your Child Improve this Skill: Ask your child to find a particular magazine that you have been reading, telling him only that it is somewhere in the house. Encourage him to search for it systematically (e.g. from room to room), rather than going from here to there without any overall search plan.

Dimension 3: Screening Information

An infant classroom is noisy – this is usually a sign of a stimulating learning environment. From amid all of this constructive noise, however, your child needs to select what he should listen to and let the rest stay in the background.

How to Help Your Child Improve this Skill: Teach him how to cross at a pelican crossing, paying special attention to the flashing 'green man'. From the child's perspective the crossing contains thousands of fascinating things to look at, but you should encourage him to focus only on the lights themselves.

Dimension 4: Disregarding Distractions

Concentration involves blocking out potential distractions. For instance, a school-aged child must be able to concentrate on the infant teacher's voice, even though there are many other noises in the classroom that could attract his attention.

How to Help your Child Improve this Skill: Ask your child to think of, say, as many different animals as he can. While he is doing this, talk to him about his favourite television programme. Encourage him to keep thinking of the different animals, even though you are saying things which may distract him.

Dimension 5: Maintaining Concentration

When your child starts school he should be able to concentrate on an educational task until it is complete. If not, he will not progress as well as he should, and he will find that he continues with an activity long after the others in the class have finished.

How to Help your Child Improve this Skill: Tell him to colour in a drawing, and time how long he persists (e.g. 2 minutes). The next night, tell him to continue with the activity for a little longer (e.g. 2 minutes 15 seconds) and give him lots of praise when he achieves this. Gradually increase the amount of time each night.

MEMORY

If your child did not have any memory at all, then he would be unable to learn; it is as simple as that. He would not learn, for instance, that water comes out of a tap, that hot items burn, that food satisfies his hunger, that a ball moves when it is kicked, and so on. Each time he did anything, it would be as though it was a completely new experience for him, and he would not build up any 'data bank' of knowledge. In school, lack of memory would mean that your child would not know where he had left his books, or what the teacher told him the previous moment. Children who have difficulties with their memory skills often experience learning problems when they start school.

Short-term and Long-term Memory

There are two parts to your child's memory. First, he has a short-term memory. Like a clerk in an office, short-term memory processes all new information that your child sees, hears, tastes, smells and touches. Everything goes into his short-term memory, which either decides that it is important information to be kept or that it is unimportant and should be forgotten. Once this decision has been made, long-term memory comes into operation. Like a filing cabinet in an office, your child's long-term memory stores information for use at a later date. If it is not stored in long-term memory, then it is lost for good.

Can you remember the colour of the car that was in front of you this morning on your way to work? Probably not, because although you were aware of the car's colour at the time – so that you would not bump into it – you did not need to remember it afterwards. But you probably do remember the day you started your first job, or the day your child celebrated his first birthday, because these were special experiences which were significant for you and were therefore stored in your long-term memory.

Psychologists have found that:

- **There is a limit to the capacity of short-term memory.** Ask your child to listen to the following string of numbers, telling him that he is to try and say them back to you as soon as you are finished: 8 3 6 2 0 1 2 3 5 8 8. He cannot possibly recall all of them.

- **There is no limit to the capacity of long-term memory.** Long-term memory is like a bottomless pit which can never become completely full. You can always remember new things.

- **Short-term memory is adversely affected by interruptions.** Using memory does require a degree of concentration. For instance, try to remember a new 10-digit telephone number while reciting the alphabet backwards – now that's difficult!

- **Long-term memory often lasts.** You probably have certain memories from your own childhood – pleasant or otherwise – even though these are memories of events that occurred many years ago.

- **Parts of long-term memory are time-limited.** There appears to be some information which enters long-term memory for several days (such as the name of a television programme you enjoyed) and then is forgotten completely.

- **Repetition improves memory.** You probably know to say something over and over again, if it has to be remembered. That is why you will keep repeating information until you are confident you know it.

- **Attention affects memory.** It does not matter how good your child's memory is, he will not be able to use it unless he is able to concentrate long enough on new pieces of information.

Adult vs Child Memory

The most obvious difference between your memory capacity and your child's memory capacity is that you can remember much more than he. For instance, if someone tells you a shopping list once, you may well be able to recall it a few minutes later, whereas your young child will forget the list almost as soon as he hears it. Between early childhood and adulthood, the ability to remember increases noticeably.

One reason for this increase is that, as memories accumulate and are stored in your long-term memory, they provide a structure in which to store later memories. It is as though once your memory's filing system is established, new memories can be retained more easily. For instance, you will be able to remember the choice of vegetables at your local supermarket more easily than your child can remember, because you have previous memories of buying these vegetables, cooking them and eating them, and this has given you a structure in which to integrate subsequent new memories. On the other hand, your child does not have these earlier experiences and therefore memorizing the range of vegetables is much harder for him.

The second reason that an adult's memory capacity is larger than a child's is that adults have learned to use memory techniques to improve their powers of retention. For instance, if you are told a telephone number verbally and are unable to write it down straight away, you will probably repeat to yourself over and over until you are confident that you have remembered it. Children aged 5 years and under rarely repeat things to themselves in this way. This is a skill that usually needs to be taught.

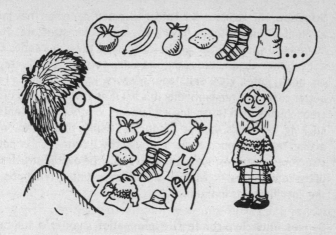

How to Improve your Child's Memory

Memory can be improved, whether you are 5 years old or 50. Here are some ways to help your child increase his memory. He can practise these himself, once you have shown him how to use them.

1. **Repetition.** One of the most effective ways to improve memory is through the use of repetition. This method is also known as 'over-learning' – in other words, your child repeats and repeats the information he wants to learn, until it is firmly established. Repetition is tedious by nature, yet it does work. It is particularly useful for remembering information that has to be recalled quickly. For instance, if your child is told by his teacher to ask the school secretary for a red pencil, he is more likely to remember this instruction if he says it over and over to himself while he walks down the corridor to the school office. Repetition stops the memory trace from fading, at least until a few minutes after the repetition stops.

2. **Structure.** Things are much harder to remember when they are all jumbled up, without having any particular structure. For instance, if your child is told by his teacher to fetch a series of items from the cupboard at the end of the corridor (pencil, crayon, book, jotter, glue, sellotape, scissors, knife), he has a far better chance of remembering this list if he divides it into discreet chunks (that is, writing implements, cutting implements, sticking materials, paper products). Using this technique makes the task much easier because the information is now structured clearly – once your child recalls the overall structure of the four groups, he will find that he immediately remembers the specific items in them.

3. **Senses.** Your child can receive information through a number of sensory channels. He can hear an instruction, he can see a series of numbers that are written down on paper, he can smell a specific odour, he can taste a specific flavour, and he can feel a specific contour. It stands to reason that he is more likely to remember a piece of information when it is transmitted to him through more than one channel, such as if he reads it, hears it, says it out loud to himself and writes or draws it as well. This multi-sensory approach to remembering and recalling does not come naturally to children, but your child can develop this technique with your encouragement.

4. **Imagery.** Young children rarely use visual imagery spontaneously as part of their memory, but they can be taught this technique. One way is to imagine a familiar scene (such as a room in your home) but incorporating the objects to be remembered. Give your child a list of four things you want to buy at the supermarket (such as a tin of soup, packet of soap powder, loaf of bread and pint of milk). To help him remember these unconnected items, he could imagine a scarecrow with a head that is a packet of soap powder, a body that is a loaf of bread, holding a pint of milk in one hand and a tin of soup in the other. With practice he will enjoy using this technique and will find it effective.

5. **Rote.** Learning by rote ('off by heart') used to be a popular technique in infant classes for helping pupils retain key pieces of information, such as the words of a song or multiplication tables. Although it is not used widely nowadays, it remains an efficient way of committing to memory essential segments of information. Pick a song that you would like your child to sing, and ask him to learn five verses. This will seem an impossible task to him at first, but if he learns one line at a time – until he can recite it by rote without having to think about it – then he will soon learn the whole song, and will be able to sing it to you without any difficulty.

LEARNING STYLE

Every child has his own distinctive way of learning. One child might always be the first with an answer to the teacher's question, giving his answer before he has fully thought out all the possible alternative answers. This impulsive learning style often leads the child to give an incorrect response. Another child might prefer to reflect more on the question before committing himself, despite his desire to offer the correct answer. This reflective learning style is more likely to lead the child to the right response.

Learning style also affects a child's progress within school. For instance, a child who is learning to read has a variety of ways he can interpret a particular word and, until he becomes a proficient reader, he has to think about these different interpretations before reading the word aloud. The dimension of reflective-impulsive learning style becomes relevant at this point. One research study assessed a group of children who were about to learn to read, in terms of how reflective or impulsive they were. When the children's progress with reading was assessed a year later, the researchers found that children who had been assessed as having a reflective learning style at age 6 were better readers a year later, compared to the children who had been assessed as having an impulsive learning style.

That is why it is important to encourage your child to take his time when working on an educational activity. Reassure him that it is better to get the right answer than it is to be the first to answer – accuracy is better than speed. Encourage him to check over his work even though he is satisfied that it is correct, and to think about his responses in class before he makes them. In the long term this will benefit his learning in the infant class.

SUMMARY

Your child's progress through the infant school curriculum depends on his learning skills (intelligence), although psychologists disagree whether these skills are inherited or acquired. Either way there are a number of things your child is expected to manage by the time he starts school, and you can help teach him them during the pre-school years. When doing so, however, it is important to make learning fun – otherwise you will make your child anxious, and he will not learn when that happens.

Concentration is also a vital part of the learning process in school. A child who cannot concentrate will not make good progress in the infant class. The ability to concentrate has five key dimensions which you can help your child to develop.

Similarly, memory is connected with learning. There is a difference between short-term and long-term memory, and also a difference between the memory skills of a child and the memory skills of an adult. You can help improve your child's memory by teaching him techniques such as the use of repetition, structure, imagery and rote. He will also benefit in the infant class by having a reflective learning style rather than an impulsive learning style.

7

THE 'THREE RS'

THE DEVELOPMENT OF READING

Children learn to read at different ages and different stages – one child might be able to read some single words by the time she starts infant school, while another might not reach that stage until the end of the first term. At home, though, learning to read should not be a formal process.

Your child's interest in books starts early on in her life, stimulated by the wide range of language-based activities she experiences during the pre-school years. The stories you read to her, the songs you sing to her, the nursery rhymes you say to her – all these help to develop her interest in spoken and written language. And this lays the foundation for her later reading ability. (Many of these activities are mentioned earlier in this book; see chapters 3 and 4.)

By the age of 3 or 4 years you will find that when you sit your child beside you in order to read her a story she will look closely at the page with the printed words on it. Already she has begun to realize there is a connection between these strange shapes and the words you read to her, and she may even point out to you that the same word appears in several places. This is a demonstration of her ability to match words of the same shape and length, an essential pre-reading skill; encourage her to do this, and read the word to her when she matches it correctly with the same word further down the page. She may also start to pick out and identify familiar signs in her surroundings (e.g. your street name, a sign for a car park, etc.). These early successes will boost her confidence with reading.

Once you find that she is looking at a book closely when you read to her, point to each word as you read it aloud. This helps her establish the notion that reading goes from left to right. But do not force her to point along with you – she will do this when she is ready. Eventually she may try to read one or two familiar words without your help.

Pre-reading Activities

Here are some useful pre-reading activities for your child at this age:

- **rhymes.** She will love repeating nursery rhymes over and over again (e.g. 'This little piggy', 'Ring-a-ring-o-roses'), or acting out rhymes (e.g. 'I'm a little teapot', 'Incy Wincy spider').

- **story discussion.** Once you have finished reading a story to her, talk about the plot, the central characters and the reasons why she liked (or disliked) that particular story. Listen to what she says to you.

- **memory games.** There are lots of memory games, such as 'the tray game' (where you show your young child a tray with four objects on it, then she has to recall them when the tray is removed), or matched pairs (with three or four pairs of cards).

- **listening activities.** This could include identifying everyday actions from a tape recording of their sounds, repeating a clapped rhythm, or asking her to close her eyes and guess who is speaking.

- **sequencing.** Remembering lists of items (e.g. 'When I went to the market I bought a...'), songs involving recall of sequences (e.g. 'Ten green bottles'), or following instructions with two pieces of information are all helpful.

- **looking games.** These include dominoes, elementary card games (e.g. snap), sorting objects into small groups according to specific features (e.g. colour, size, shape) and copying basic shapes from cards.

- **matching.** She benefits from playing matching games such as word-lotto. At this stage she will make comparisons only on the basis of the overall word shape, but that is a central pre-reading skill.

- **page-turning.** Although she cannot yet read, you can involve her in the reading process by asking her to turn the page at the appropriate moment. This focuses her attention on the printed page.

Reading should always be enjoyable, so avoid the temptation to pressurize your child into guessing at reading; that may make her so anxious that she tenses every time a book is brought out. Choose books for her that are bright, well illustrated and at a level of interest suitable for a child her age. The formal teaching of reading will be carried out at school, but your child will have a head start if she already enjoys reading-related activities and is confident completing them. By the time she starts infant school, however, she should be able to recognize her own name if she sees it written somewhere.

Reading Problems

Parents often worry that a left-handed child is likely to be a slow reader, but there is no evidence to support this. There have been numerous investigations into this and they all have reached the same finding – children who are left-handed score just as highly on reading tests as children of the same age who are right-handed. So there is no need to become filled with anxiety when you realize your child prefers to use her left hand for drawing and writing. Certainly you should not try to force her to use her right hand instead, as that could lead to problems where none existed before.

Every child learns to read at her own rate and you should not be concerned if there are others in her infant class who are further ahead with reading than she is. However, there are some children who are very bright and articulate and who are able to communicate their ideas verbally yet who have great difficulty learning to read. This condition – known as 'dyslexia' or 'specific learning difficulty' – is estimated to occur in up to 5 per cent of all children. Boys are more affected than girls, in the ratio of 4:1.

Dyslexia – which can range from mild to severe – was first detected over 90 years ago but there is still no general agreement on the cause. Some believe that it is a genetic condition passed down from parent to child, whereas others link it to an abnormality of the child's nervous system. Regardless of the cause of dyslexia, accurate identification is very important in order that the child can receive specialist help. Although proper assessment for the condition must be carried out by a psychologist (usually when a child has been at school for a year or two), there is be some evidence that signs of dyslexia can be seen under the age of 5. The chart below lists the main features to look for.

Area of Development	Pre-school Signs of Dyslexia
Movement and Balance	Difficulty dressing independently Late learning to fasten shoe-laces or buttons Problems putting correct shoe on each foot Excessive tripping, and bumping into things Difficulty catching, throwing and kicking a ball
Speech and Language	Slow to learn to speak clearly Consistently calls colours by wrong names Jumbled phrases regularly (e.g. 'beddy tear') Confusion with words indicating directions Struggles to clap the beat of a simple rhyme Lisps during the pre-school years
Memory and Sequencing	Problems remembering sequences Poor recall of familiar nursery rhymes Difficulty remembering names of everyday objects Confusion between left and right Difficulty selecting odd one out of rhyming sequence Mixes up time sequences of a typical day
General Development	Often inattentive Problems following instructions At times seems to 'search' for the right word Is uninterested in pre-reading activities, preferring instead creative (non-verbal) activities, such as painting

Not all dyslexic children exhibit all of these feature. And many pre-school children who are not dyslexic make the same sorts of mistakes and have the same sorts of problems. For instance, there are plenty of children who cannot follow instructions, or who cannot name colours accurately, yet they learn to read without any difficulty. So if your child has some of the features mentioned in the chart above, this does not mean she is dyslexic. These minor problems will probably vanish by the time she starts infant school, or a few months later.

Some professionals claim that what differentiates the dyslexic pre-schooler from the non-dyslexic pre-schooler is not just the presence of these features, but also their severity (i.e. the difficulties are marked), their clarity (i.e. the difficulties are very noticeable, even to the untrained eye), and their persistence (i.e. the difficulties remain for much longer than would normally be expected). If you think that your child may be dyslexic, voice your fears to her class teacher.

THE DEVELOPMENT OF WRITING

Writing is one of the things that we do as adults without even thinking about it. Yet it is a very complex skill, one that starts to develop right from the moment your child is born. Good hand control, accurate vision, concentration and an understanding of language are all crucial elements of neat writing.

Much of your child's play during her first year contributes towards her later writing skills because it involves manipulating toys and exploring them with her fingers and hands – this extends her hand control. By the age of 12 months she grasps a pencil or crayon and tries to make a mark on a piece of paper; by 18 months she scribbles freely and at the age of 2 years she scribbles in a more coordinated way, using long straight lines instead of the haphazard strokes she used previously – she might even make a reasonable attempt at copying a vertical line. The typical 3-year-old child copies a circle, using a pencil or crayon.

Between 3 and 5 years, hand control and overall

development improve to the point where your child is ready to move away from copying shapes. Now she can try drawing patterns that require her to take the pencil off the paper and then to continue at another point close by; this is a basic feature of writing.

Pre-Writing Activities

Here are some useful pre-writing activities for your child at this age:

- **drawing.** Encourage your child to draw anything at all, and be prepared to give suggestions, such as 'Mummy' or 'a house'. You could even start the drawing, then let her complete it. Praise her efforts.

- **colouring.** Practice at colouring in a basic shape or a drawing with a clear solid outline allows your child's hand-control to become more controlled. At first she will colour over the lines, but she becomes neater as she progresses.

- **dot-to-dot patterns.** Make up a simple dot-to-dot pattern (e.g. a circle shape with six dots), and ask your child to join them together. These exercises give her practice in drawing in an organized manner.

- **tracing.** This can be very difficult, so start with a very elementary outline (e.g. a square) then progress to more difficult ones. Eventually she can try tracing letter shapes, even though she does not realize what these shapes are.

- **pattern completion.** Draw a wavy line halfway across the page and then ask your child to complete it. You can provide top and bottom guidelines if that helps her keep a straight line. Vary the pattern each time.

- **sand play.** Children love drawing in the sand. If you have access to a sand tray, draw a shape in the sand and ask your child to copy it. Suggest that she makes patterns and drawings of her own in the sand.

- **scribbling books.** Do not forget to give her plenty of time for good old-fashioned scribbling. Every child likes doodling on a piece of blank paper, without having anything specific to draw.

- **maze puzzles.** You may be able to buy a puzzle book containing simple mazes for a young child. Finding her way out of the maze with her pencil along the paper encourages directionality and hand control.

Pencil grip is important too. Although your child can make a good drawing no matter how she holds the pencil, she will need a more precise grip in order to complete many of these pre-writing activities and also for writing itself. You may have to show her how to do this. Put a pencil in her hand so that she grips it between her thumb and first finger, then place her second finger in position so that it supports the pencil approximately ½ – 1 inch from the tip. This takes plenty of practice!

Although there are some children who are able to read sentences when they start school, far fewer are able to write neatly. Most children do not achieve neat writing until they around 7 years old, although your child will probably be able to write her own name when she begins in the infant class. Help her achieve this particular target by writing her name, then letting her trace it, or by making dot-to-dot patterns that she can then join together to form the letters of her name. Use blank paper so that she is not bothered about keeping within lines.

Writing Problems

Children vary in the speed at which they learn to write; girls usually acquire a neat handwriting style before boys. Try not to make your child anxious about her writing ability, as that could make matters worse. Very often a child's writing is scrawly and poorly formed simply because she is not ready to write neatly. The best strategy is to give her lots of practice, but in short episodes lasting only 2 or 3 minutes each time.

Do not worry if your child is left-handed – she will still learn to write neatly. A child whose parents make an issue of the fact that she writes using her left hand will have a low level of self-confidence and may start to become anxious about writing, afraid that she will never achieve the neatness of a right-handed writer – and this, of course, is completely untrue. Accept her left-handedness, just as you accept her other characteristics. This is far better than building a source of confrontation between you.

Having said this, English writing patterns – going from left to right – do favour the right-handed pupil and involve movements that come naturally to a right-handed child. There are specific strategies to help your left-handed child learn to write:

- **Avoid fountain pens and felt-tip pens.** These inks are slow-drying, and she may smudge her writing because her hand moves across the words after she writes them (if right-handed, her hand would move in front of the words).

- **Avoid sharp pencils.** When writing, she pushes the pencil from one side of the page to the other (unlike a right-handed child who drags it across), and this can cause the paper to tear or the tip of the pencil to break if it is too sharp.

- **Let her sit comfortably.** Watch your child as she writes – she probably positions her body differently from a child who is right-handed. This is perfectly normal and is nothing to worry about. Just make sure she is comfortable.

- **Ensure good body posture.** There is no need for a left-handed pupil to sit sprawled or hunched over her written work; if she does, it has less to with being left-handed and more to do with poor body posture.

NUMBER DEVELOPMENT

Your child starts to use numbers as part of her everyday vocabulary long before she actually understands what they signify. By the age of 3 you may even see her point to objects and try to count them – but she will not get it right (unless she makes a lucky guess, of course).

This is followed by the next stage of number development, at around 3 or 4 years, when she begins to match different groups with the same number of objects in them. For example, give her a small pile of 4 blue bricks, a small pile of 5 yellow bricks, a small pile of 4 green bricks, and a small pile of 6 black bricks; point to the 4 blue bricks and ask her to find a pile with the same number of bricks in it. Her ability to do this correctly is a demonstration of her understanding that a number represents a specific quantity and that it corresponds to a group of items.

The next step in the development of number is your child's realization that numbers also follow a fixed sequence. Parents often assume that because they themselves know that the number 3 comes after the number 2, and so on, that this is very obvious. But your child has to learn this – it is not immediately obvious. She will learn the sequence of numbers from one to five before any other sequence.

At this stage she also begins to grasp the language of number, such as 'big/little', 'more/less'. The typical 3-year-old can make simple size comparisons. Give her a large glass of juice and a small glass of juice, and ask her to point to the big glass. She should be able to make this distinction without much difficulty. And by the age of 4 she will have the first stage of mature counting. Place four of the same objects in front of her (e.g. sweets), then ask her to count them out, pointing to each one as she does so – she may complete this accurately.

When your child starts the infant class she should be able to recognize the numbers up to 10, or perhaps up to 20, and count at least up to 7. She will probably have an idea about the different time phases of the average day, and will know that breakfast comes before lunch, that dinner comes at the end of the day, and so on. Your child may also be able to identify a couple of coins, even though she does not understand their value.

Pre-Number Activities

Here are some useful pre-number activities for your child at this age:

- **dice games.** Whether it is snakes and ladders or ludo, dice games are very helpful because they help establish a link between the number of dots on the dice and the number of times she can move her game piece.

- **setting the table.** Put out several saucers on the table, then ask your child to put a cup on top of each one. This concept of one-to-one correspondence underlies the development of number.

- **time sequences.** Encourage her to be aware of the different time sequences that occur throughout the day, such as when her brother comes home from school, or when she has a break for juice and biscuits.

- **number recognition.** Draw your child's attention to numbers that appear in her immediate environment, such as the numbers on the clock, the pages on her books, or on the poster on her bedroom wall.

- **writing numbers.** Give her practice writing the numbers. At first you will need to write them out so that she can copy them, but eventually she will be able to write them herself without prompting from you.

- **counting exercises.** Lots of routine activities can involve counting, and these can be used to encourage your child's interest in number – such as counting the stairs as she climbs them, or counting the number of items you have bought at the shop.

- **coin recognition.** Pick one or two coins (e.g. the one-pence and two-pence coins) and let her become familiar with them. Then place a one-pence coin in with other (different) coins, and ask her to pick it out.

- **number rhymes.** Young children generally love number rhymes (e.g. 'five currant buns', 'five little speckled frogs'), and this can be a fun way of teaching number sequences.

Number Problems

Like reading and writing, number is a concept children grasp at their own rate. Certainly, difficulties with learning to count are less frequent than difficulties with reading and writing. In many instances number difficulties are caused by parents expecting too much of their child during the pre-school years.

Psychological research has shown that children perceive their world in a way that reflects their limited thought processes, and this affects their understanding of number. For example, a child under the age of 5 tends to focus on one part of a number-related problem only. Try this: show your young child two pieces of modelling clay that are rolled into balls of the same size. Confirm that she agrees they are of equal size. Then, while she is looking at you, roll one of the balls into a thin, sausage shape. She will probably focus on the length of the rolled piece and tell you that it now has more in it than the ball-shaped piece. Only when she reaches school age will she realize that although the piece of clay is longer, it is also thinner.

This is a natural feature of her pre-school development. Even if you find her responses frustrating and difficult to comprehend in a problem-solving task like this, there is nothing you can do about. She will mature in her own time, at her own pace. Your annoyance at her limited grasp of number-related concepts will not improve her understanding, and may cause problems when she eventually starts school.

SUMMARY

Every child learns to read, write and count at her own rate. But there are lots of things you can do to help develop her pre-reading skills, her pre-writing skills and her pre-number skills, before she sets foot in the infant class. Many children experience difficulties in learning these basic aspects of the curriculum, but few experience severe ones. However, if your child does have a persistent learning difficulty in the infant class, especially with reading, then raise the matter with her teacher and seek specialist help.

The 'Right' Infant School

8

CHOOSING AN INFANT SCHOOL

You now have some freedom of choice when it comes to choosing which infant school you would like your child to attend, whereas previously your child had to attend the local authority school closest to home. This rule was totally inflexible. Parents who wanted their child to register at a specific infant school which was not in their area literally had to move house. And there were plenty of families prepared to do this – stories abounded about families who bought a house 100 metres along the street from the house they previously lived in, just so their child could go to another school.

A change in the rules concerned with parent participation in education means that parents can exercise choice when selecting their child's school. Quite simply, you can apply for your child to attend any local authority school you want, subject to reasonable limitations – for example, that the school is not already full, or that your child's presence will not have an adverse effect on the educational progress of the other pupils. Of course, you will have to consider how your child will get to the infant school of your choice (he should not have to become involved in complex transport arrangements), but if you live in a major city then you will be within reasonable travelling distance of perhaps four or five local education authority schools.

CHOOSING THE LOCAL SCHOOL

Even though you do have freedom of choice now, you will probably opt for the infant school nearest to your home – and for sound reasons:

- **He will know lots of children who start school with him.** Your child will be happier and more confident knowing that several of his friends, or children he met in nursery, will be in his class.

- **His siblings are already at that school.** You will have a hard job taking and collecting your children each day if they are all at different schools, and there could be a clash in programmes of school events.

- **It fits in more conveniently with your own routine.** You may be dependent on having a conveniently situated infant school in order for you to get out to work on time yourself each morning.

- **You know people who can give you an informed view of the school.** Friends and neighbours probably also send their children to that school, so you can easily find out accurate information about it.

BACKGROUND KNOWLEDGE

Your own first-hand contact with a school is essential before forming a final opinion about its suitability for your child. But you should also try to gain as much background information as possible, preferably before you actually visit the school. This information can be gathered from a variety of sources, including:

- **other parents whose children attend the school.** Every parent has his or her own view of a school, and what suits one child might not suit another. However, talking to other parents will provide 'consumer opinion' and may help to identify the school's strengths as well as its weaknesses. Bear in mind, though, that one parent might be delighted because a school teaches music, while another parent of a child at the same school might be annoyed because this means her child spends less time working on reading, writing, spelling and numbers.

- **other children who attend the school.** Ask any child about his school and it is a sure bet that he will have some complaint to make! Even so, children are often able to give a reasonably accurate account of what goes on inside a school, the things that parents are not often aware of – like the infant teacher who constantly shouts at pupils but who smiles sweetly at their parents when they arrive to collect their children, or the teacher who seems boring when talking to parents yet stimulates the pupils' imaginations during drama classes and at storytime.

- **the school brochure.** Every school, in every local authority, produces a brochure or handbook describing the school's facilities, the curriculum, hours of opening, staffing levels, holiday periods, support services, educational philosophy and so on. These brochures are intended to promote a positive image of the school, and although they might not provide a totally accurate reflection of school life they do contain lots of useful information. School brochures are available to anyone who asks for a copy. Each school issues and distributes its own brochure.

ARRANGING A VISIT

The best way to know what is really going on in a school is to visit it personally; if you are choosing between a number of potential infant schools you should visit each one in turn. Although this can take days, look on it positively – schooling is a vital part of your child's life, and during his school years he will spend more of his waking hours in the company of the pupils and teachers than he will being with you at home. Try to find time to visit all the schools in your area so that you can create an informed impression rather than relying on hearsay, third-party perceptions or your own memories of schooling.

Having decided to make a visit, contact the school in plenty of time, probably at least one term before your child is due to enrol. Speak to the headteacher, explain why you are calling, and arrange a time that suits both of you. You should receive a positive response. As some schools organize open days for parents to look round and talk to members of staff, the school's secretary might suggest that you take advantage of this opportunity before having a personal interview with the headteacher, and this would be an acceptable approach. However, you will still want to speak to the headteacher after you have been there for the open day.

If you have a choice, leave your child with someone else when you visit the school for the first time, even though he desperately wants to go along with you. You will be able to focus your thoughts more during the visit if you do not have to worry about your child's behaviour – children have an amazing knack of behaving immaturely when their parents want them to behave sensibly. A parent of a prospective pupil visiting a school should not hurry. Allow plenty of time for a good look round, probably about an hour. This will leave you time to ask questions, to speak to staff and to consider the work that the pupils are doing in the class.

10 Questions to Ask on a School Visit

Different parents use different criteria when judging whether or not a particular school is a 'good' one. For instance, some are concerned about the reading scheme used in the infant department, while others may be more interested in, say, sporting activities and other extra-curricular classes. However, here are 10 key questions that you should always ask:

1. **Who will be teaching my child?** In some schools, teachers are not allocated a class for the next session until just before the summer break. However, if the teacher of your child's class has not been selected yet, speak to the teacher of this year's infant class. Find out everything you can about the activities she provides for her pupils, including arts and crafts, drama, science and PE. You will soon form an opinion about the teacher while talking to her. If you do not like her very much (for example because she is too authoritarian), then your child is unlikely to enjoy being in her class.

2. **How many other teachers are there in the whole school?**
   Remember that your child will not be in the infant class for ever,
   so find out the level and structure of teaching staff throughout
   the entire school. The main points to ask about include the size
   of classes, the availability of specialist teachers (e.g. art, environmental studies), the availability of extra teaching for pupils
   with learning difficulties, and if there are any plans to expand
   the school. Now that schools have control over a substantial
   part of their own budgets, headteachers have an element of
   choice in employing additional staff.

3. **Is the school building in good condition?** Research has shown
   that pupils' educational success is partly linked to the structure
   and cleanliness of the actual school building. Of course, what
   goes on in the classroom is what matters, and you would not
   want your child to attend a brand new school if you felt the standards of teaching were unsatisfactory. However, you would not
   like to go to work every day in an office that was dreary, damp
   and visibly run down. The atmosphere would depress you and
   you would not work as hard. A decaying school building can
   have a similar effect on the pupils.

4. **How is the playground structured and monitored?** When an
   infant class is part of a larger primary school, these young
   pupils should have their own self-contained playground which
   allows play that is free from interference by older pupils. This
   will help boost your child's self-confidence and his feeling of
   security within the school. Playgrounds should have an even
   surface, without potholes or scattered rubbish, so that children
   can play with fear of unnecessary injury. It is also worth asking
   about the level of adult supervision in the playground during
   intervals.

5. **What are the academic achievements of pupils who attend the
   school?** Although you want your child to develop his personal
   and social qualities at school, you also want to know that the

school has good academic standards, that its pupils learn effectively and efficiently. However, unlike a secondary school which publishes pupils' results in formal examinations, an infant school does not have this information. You will have to form an opinion, therefore, by talking to the class teacher and headteacher, by looking at the work carried out in each class, and by asking other parents.

6. **What do infants learn, other than the 'Three Rs'?** Reading, writing and arithmetic are core aspects of the infant curriculum, and you should satisfy yourself that these are taught well. Yet your child will study other subjects too, such as environmental studies, a modern language, music and drama. These form an important part of your child's school day, so make a note of the range of different subjects offered in the school, and also when children are able to access them – there is little point in sending your child to a school because it offers drama, only to discover that he sees the drama teacher once a month.

7. **How does the school meet the special educational needs of a slow learner?** While every teacher is trained to teach a class of children who vary in their rate of learning, there are some children with learning difficulties who require additional help with learning over and above that normally available within the classroom. Every school should have a clear policy on how to meet the needs of such pupils, and it should be easy to understand by all parents. The policy should be well structured, with clear aims and clearly designated resources.

8. **How are computers used in the classroom?** The typical classroom computer can give your child access to a whole new range of educational opportunities if it is used properly as part of the infant class curriculum. The problem is that a computer will sit untouched in a corner of the classroom unless the school has a systematic policy on micro-technology and unless the teacher knows how to use it. Check out the situation in each

111

school you visit. Computers can also be used as word processors to help children in their writing activities – they can also correct spelling mistakes.

9. **What is the school's policy on discipline?** A happy school atmosphere does not occur by chance – it develops out of a strong policy on discipline. Staff should have clear rules regarding acceptable levels of behaviour, these rules should be clearly communicated to the pupils, and there should be a planned system for dealing with children who break them. But discipline also involves fostering positive relationships between pupils and between teachers and pupils, and you should look for evidence of definite strategies to achieve this goal.

10. **What is the level of parental involvement in the school?** Fortunately, schools frequently regard parents as partners in the education of their children, and therefore welcome any parental interest. There should be regular reports about your child's progress, and you should be able to speak to his teacher without too much trouble. In many schools, a class teacher or headteacher can be contacted without a prior appointment; and parents are often positively encouraged to spend time in the infant classroom, especially during the first year.

Looking Round

In addition to all these – and other – questions to ask during your visit, there is a lot you can learn simply by using your eyes. If what you see does not match up with what you are told, then believe your eyes. The chart below lists features to look for during your school visit:

Positive Features	Negative Features
Classroom walls covered with lots of varied examples of the pupils' work.	Classroom walls covered with faded and repetitive examples of pupils' work.
Books that are varied and easily accessible to the pupils.	Books that appear shabby and tattered, which are not well displayed in class.
Teachers who seem genuinely caring and interested in the pupils.	Teachers who seem bored and who are hostile towards the pupils.
Noise in the classroom that stems from groups of pupils working together.	Noise that stems from pupil boredom and poor discipline.
Children who are working on an assignment independently.	Children who are constantly out of their seats asking the teacher for help.
A play area in the classroom that is tidy and amply stocked.	A dreary play area that is untidy, dirty and contains only a few toys.

Having covered all these matters in your visit to the school, coupled with all the background information you have gathered, you are at last in a position to make an informed choice. But if you are still uncertain, think about the issues that are troubling you, and perhaps make a second visit before making a final decision about which school is the right one for your child.

PRIVATE DAY SCHOOLS AND
BOARDING SCHOOLS

All the points mentioned throughout this chapter also apply when you are considering sending your child to a private day school or boarding school – do not assume that all aspects of every private school are of a high standard simply because parents pay for their children to attend there. (There are those parents who maintain that some teachers only survive in private schools because the pupils are usually selected on intellectual ability, and therefore are more capable and are more independent learners.) So be prepared to carry out the same information-gathering exercise as you would for any infant school.

There is more uniformity among local authority infant classes than there is among the infant classes of private schools. Whereas virtually all local authority schools aim to provide an equivalent education for their pupils, private schools often have individual educational policies. For instance, one private school might cater for the needs of pupils with very high educational potential, with a focus on good exam results, while another might focus on enhancing the personal development of its pupils, with an emphasis on fostering pupil contentment. You have to decide for yourself which philosophy is the one for your child.

You may want to consider a residential boarding school, although most parents tremble at the thought of sending their infant away from home at such a young age. Nevertheless, this option may be necessary, perhaps because you work abroad for much of the time. At boarding school a child has to cope with being away from home for long periods, as well as getting to know the way of life there – and this can make starting school doubly difficult. Research suggests that bullying in residential schools is high; younger pupils are bullied more. Many boarding schools allow pupils to attend on a non-residential daily basis.

SUMMARY

You will probably have a choice of conveniently-located infant schools for your child; therefore it is important that you make an informed choice based on accurate knowledge. You can gain useful background information by talking to other parents and children who attend there. However, the best way to choose a school for your child is to visit all the alternatives. During your visit to the school there are specific features you should inquire about, including who your child's teacher will be, the curriculum, the level of staffing, the use of computer technology and so on. This also applies even though you may be sending your child to a private school or boarding school.

STARTING INFANT SCHOOL

9

COUNTDOWN TO THE FIRST DAY

There is plenty to do in preparation for your child's first day at infant school. Do not leave everything to the last minute or you and your child will be rushed and harassed. Advance planning and preparation are essential if things are to go smoothly on that all-important day. The timetable below will help you get organized.

COUNTDOWN TO THE FIRST DAY IN THE INFANT CLASS

- **1 year before:**
  Make a comprehensive list of all the local infant schools in your area, and select the ones that you might possibly want your child to attend.

- **10 months before:**
  Start to gather background information about the various schools from other parents whose children go there and from the children themselves.

- **9 months before:**
  Phone all the schools on your 'possible' list, and ask them to send you out their school brochures – updated versions should be available by then.

- **8 months before:**
  Using the information you have gathered together so far, try to reduce the list of possible schools down to perhaps only three or four.

- **7 months before:**
  Arrange to visit the schools on your list. Try to make all the visits within a two-week period so that the details of each stay fresh in your mind, to help you make comparisons.

- **6 months before:**
  Choose the infant school for your child, and register her there. You may see an announcement in your local paper advising parents of registration dates and times.

- **5 months before:**
  Having made your choice, now is the time to let your child know which school she will be going to. Tell her all the positive reasons for your choice.

- **4 months before:**
  Arrange for her to visit her new school. The chances are, however, that the school already has a day organized for new pupils starting the infant class.

- **3 months before:**
  Start talking about her new school more frequently, reminding her that she will be leaving her nursery or playgroup quite soon.

- **2 months before:**
  Now is the time for her to say her goodbyes to the carers in her pre-school provision – they will probably organize a farewell party for all the 'leavers', including her.

- **6 weeks before:**
  Start buying the clothes that she will need. Most schools issue parents with a list of clothing requirements – you should stick reasonably closely to that.

- **5 weeks before:**
  You will probably know some of the other children who will be in your child's class – invite a few of them over to your house so that she can get to know them before school starts.

- **4 weeks before:**
  Take your child with you when you buy her first schoolbag, pencils and stationery. Let her make the final choice herself, where possible.

- **3 weeks before:**
  Decide what you are going to do about lunches (i.e. school lunch or packed lunch). If she is taking a packed lunch, buy her a lunch box that she is happy with.

- **2 weeks before:**
  Make sure you write her name – or sew on name labels – on every single piece of clothing that she intends to wear to school, to minimize losses.

- **12 days before:**
  Buy her an alarm clock that will be used to wake her up in the mornings when she starts school. Practise using this so that she gets used to the sound of the alarm waking her.

- **11 days before:**
  Make a small 'countdown to school' calendar for your child, so that she can tick off the remaining days as they go past. This helps foster her enthusiasm.

- **10 days before:**
  Take a practice walk along the route between home and school, in order to familiarize her and also to time how long the journey actually takes.

- **7 days before:**
  Make a final check of her clothes, pencils, lunch box, schoolbag and so on, in case there is something that you might have missed.

- **5 days before:**
  Your child may want to stay for school lunch along with the other children. Have a week's supply of the exact money that she will need to pay for school meals.

- **4 days before:**
  Let her practise putting on and taking off the clothes she will change into for PE (probably only plimsolls) – help her become skilled in this.

- **3 days before:**
  Discuss with your child the sort of snack foods that she would like to eat in school during the intervals, and buy a few of these to have ready for her.

- **2 days before:**
  If possible, go on an outing with your child and have fun together – that will help her stay relaxed rather than becoming too focused on starting school.

- **1 day before:**
  Do not do anything overly demanding or exciting. Better to have a calm day at home, laying out her school clothes, etc., ready for the next day.

- **The night before:**
  Put her to bed at her usual bedtime, even though she may claim to be too excited to go to sleep straight away. She will nod off eventually, despite her protests.

Principles for Planning

The list above is only a guideline, as is the time scale, but it does identify the main tasks you have to complete. Your preparation will go more smoothly if you also keep to the following principles:

- **Involve your child when making minor decisions.** She should be allowed to make minor choices about school-related matters, such as what schoolbag or lunch box to use, what pencils to buy, and so on. This will increase her enthusiasm for starting school.

- **Make sure shopping for school is enjoyable.** Taking your young child out shopping with you can be trying at the best of times, never mind when she is excited. Try not to rush round hurriedly, however, or else the buying trips will become something of a chore rather than a pleasure.

- **Tell her what you are doing.** She will want you to keep her informed – for instance that you are going to visit a school, that you have decided on a particular school, that she will be visiting the school herself, etc. Your child is interested in all these matters.

- **Do not leave the awkward things till last.** There are bound to be a couple of items that are unavailable immediately, even though your child needs them for starting school (e.g. a particular lunch box, school shoes in her size, etc.). Try to locate these sooner rather than later.

- **Let your child voice her feelings.** As the stages of preparation proceed, your child will begin to express her feelings about starting infant school (e.g. happiness, anxiety). Listen to what she tells you and provide reassurance if she seems to be worrying.

- **Take advice from your other children.** You may be in the fortunate position of having older children at the same school already. Be willing to take their advice about the things your child will need, because they already have first-hand experience of being a pupil at the school.

- **Do not be inflexible regarding school clothes.** When a first child starts infant school, parents are often meticulous about the items of clothing specified on the school list. However, there is always flexibility – your child does not need to have absolutely everything exactly as the list describes.

- **Budget for the expense.** Children are costly, and the expense only increases every year. Given that the preparations for starting school will involve you in spending money, the best strategy is to budget for this so that you can afford to buy your child all that you want to.

SUMMARY

Another way to help your child get ready for school is for you to be properly organized. There is lots to be done in the year prior to starting the infant class, right up to the night before. Planning ahead will makes things easier for your child, and for you. Make these preparations fun, and involve your child wherever possible.

10

THE FIRST DAY

COPING WITH THE SEPARATION

Planning and preparing for the first day, as suggested in the previous chapters, is crucial in order to make your child's start in the infant class trouble-free. Yet there is one other essential aspect that you should also have prepared him for: the separation from you.

Examples

Consider the following two children, Donna and Gary. They both joined their new infant class on the same day, along with several other children. But this is as far as the similarity went. Since that first day Donna has been having a marvellous time – from the moment when she said goodbye to her mum and dad on the threshold of the infant classroom she has relished every minute of her short time in school. She has settled in well, made lots of new friends, and loves telling her parents her news when they meet her at the end of the school day.

Sadly, however, Gary's school experience has been quite different. He cried painfully on the first day, desperately clinging to his mum, not wanting to let go of her hand. Gary has never found it easy to separate temporarily from his parents, and the start to infant school simply highlighted this. Even now, several weeks after term began, he cries each morning as he watches his mother walk away from him out through the school gates.

Unlike Donna, Gary has not had much pre-school experience of separating from his parents, mainly because he created such a fuss when leaving them. And, rather than having to deal with his tears and tantrums, his parents deliberately limited the number of times they left him in the care of someone else. This solved the problem in the short term, but has caused long-term difficulties that are now showing up in school.

Helpful Activities

You must try to get your child used to short temporary separations from you, before he has to cope with the major and regular separation when he joins the infant class. There are many different opportunities for achieving this during the pre-school years, including:

- **nursery or playgroup.** Attendance at any form of pre-school establishment – whether a nursery, playgroup, parent-and-toddler group or crèche – will allow your child to experience separation from you in an informal, but supervised, situation. Research indicates that children who have used these pre-school opportunities cope better with the infant class separation.

- **babysitters.** Of course, you use a babysitter for your own benefit, to enable you to go out for the evening without your child. But this also has a positive spin-off for your child – it helps him become accustomed to being separated from you while he remains in the safe, familiar environment of his own home. The use of an experienced babysitter helps all of you.

- **leisure activities.** The range of leisure opportunities for young children is limitless – there are dancing groups, gymnastic classes, swimming lessons, and so on. All of these provide your child with a new source of stimulation and a chance to manage on his own without you holding his hand. And the supervising adults can settle him if he does become upset.

- **playing with a friend.** Your child is more likely to cope with a short separation from you if he is left with familiar people. The excitement of going over to a friend's house to play, coupled with the fact that his friend is there when you drop him off, increases his self-confidence and makes him feel less dependent on you.

Separation Action Plan

Having identified a suitable opportunity for a temporary separation from your child during the pre-school years along the lines suggested, the following 10-Point Action Plan offers guidelines for managing this experience effectively. (These suggestions also apply when leaving your child on his first day in infant school):

1. **Tell your child in advance.** Do not conceal the separation from your child until the last moment – that gives him no chance to prepare psychologically for something that may be quite difficult for him, nor is it likely to strengthen his trust in you. So tell him in advance that he will be playing at his best friend's house tomorrow, or that he will be attending gymnastics this afternoon.

2. **Provide reassurance.** Whether or not he has difficulty coping with these separations from you, reassure him anyway that he will be happy and safe when you are not with him. A few words may be all that is needed to make him feel calm and confident.

Be careful, however, not to overdo it, or else you might actually make him feel anxious when no such anxiety existed before.

3. **Stay calm.** Worry is contagious, particularly between parents and children. In any situation that your child feels worried about, he will look to you in order to judge how anxious you are – and if he sees you are anxious this will confirm that his own fears are justified. So you have to be calm and relaxed on the outside, no matter how tense you might feel inside.

4. **Explain collection time.** Of course you are going to collect him at the end of the activity. That may seem obvious to you, but not necessarily to your child. Explain to him that you will be back again quite soon (he will not understand phrases like 'in 40 minutes' or 'in just over an hour'), and that you are looking forward to hearing about all the fun he had.

5. **Get him organized.** As your child is more vulnerable when his environment is unstructured, do not leave him until you know a responsible adult has made contact with him personally and that there is a definite course of activities for him to follow. Your child will find the separation less stressful when he knows there is an organized plan for him.

6. **Do not make the separation too long.** Assuming you have gone through all the earlier steps in this action plan, your child will be ready for the separation. There is no need to make it drawn out; instead, your child will probably find it easier if you keep goodbyes undramatic and brief, with a normal kiss on the cheek, a hug, and 'See you soon.'

7. **Do not hang about.** You may feel tempted to linger on, once the temporary separation has been made, in order to verify that your child is not upset. Fine, as long as he does not see you – if he does, then he may start to become upset. A better strategy is to think positively, convince yourself that he will be settled, and leave calmly and unhurriedly.

8. **Return on time.** Resist the desire to collect your child ahead of schedule. First, he may be thoroughly enjoying himself and reluctant to stop early. Second, he may see you waiting and insist on leaving the activity – this could cause you both embarrassment if he becomes determined to get his own way. Neither should you be late arriving to collect him, as that could upset him too.

9. **Talk to him about the activity.** Whether a babysitter or nursery, a leisure class or a friend's house, talk to your child about the activity when you meet him. Your interest and enthusiasm in the day's events will make him feel positive about it as well, and this in turn will increase his confidence for coping with separation the next time.

10. **Remind your child of previous successes.** Each time he is about to have another temporary separation from you, remind him of the previous occasions when he has been away from you, pointing out how much he enjoyed himself and how well he managed. This fosters your child's positive attitude in these instances.

Other Preparation

Other strategies for preparing your child for the start of school have been discussed in the previous chapters (particularly Chapter 3). However, it is worth mentioning again that the first day in the infant class will be so much easier for your child if he is familiar with the school. The chart below lists some things your child should have the opportunity to do on his pre-admission visit, all of which will help him later on that all-important first day.

What Your Child Should Do	Why He Should Do It
Meet his class teacher	The infant teacher will have been allocated before the end of the previous term. Meeting her will reduce your child's potential anxieties.
Sit in his classroom	To you, one classroom may be much the same as another. But to your child, each classroom is unique. So let him sit at a desk in order to 'get the feel' of the room.
See the dining area	Your young child may be worried that he won't have anywhere to eat, or that the food may not be very nice. Seeing the dining hall will reassure him—hopefully.
Use the school toilets	The school toilet area may be bigger than any he has been used to before, because it's for many children. Experience of using the toilet builds his confidence.
Meet some classmates	The chances are that he will be able to meet other children who are starting school along with him. Any potential shyness will be reduced.
Discover the class routine	Although not working to a rigid schedule, most infant classes operate to a timetable— for example storytime followed by language work, then the interval, etc.
Walk round the playground	Playtime can be a source of considerable worry for a young pupil, because the play-ground seems so vast. Walking round it will help your child feel comfortable.
Watch a PE lesson	This is a new area of the curriculum for your child, one which he may be apprehensive

about. Seeing others coping with these
activities is reassuring.

THE BIG DAY

The preparations are all over now, the curtain rises and the
show commences. Your child wakes up, full of excitement
and anticipation, ready to go. You are probably just as
excited, though with mixed emotions as your child starts
this new phase of his young life.

The first day does not always go according to plan,
despite all your preparations. No matter how many steps
you take to get your child ready for school, first day tears
are common. There are always a couple of children sobbing
when their parents take them to the classroom for the first
time at the start of term. This is a normal reaction, not one
to become worried about. There is absolutely no connection between a difficult separation from you on the first day
and your child's subsequent psychological and educational development.

The principles outlined in the Separation Action Plan
earlier – designed to help your child get used to temporary
separations during the pre-school years – are as relevant for
the first day in infant school. When you leave your home
with your child, let him see that you are calm, relaxed and
happy – even though you may be feeling slightly tearful
yourself! Despite your possible sadness at the realization
that the start of infant school means the end of an era in
both your lives, try not to show any signs of concern.

Should your child become upset at the point you leave
him – usually when he is well inside the classroom and
has spoken to the teacher – remind him that he will be fine.
Tell him that the other boys and girls will be friendly and

pleasant towards him, explain that the teacher is looking forward to having him in her class, and point out that you will be there to collect him at the end of the school day. Do not give him any indication that you are troubled, since this will only add to his agitation.

Your child has to be absolutely certain that the separation will take place whether or not he wants it to, and that his tears (if he does cry) will not change anything. Be determined to see your plan of action through. He will accept your reassurances once he realizes you mean what you say. Try not to linger unnecessarily on the threshold of the classroom. Leave promptly even though your child may appear upset – he will be fine. Make sure that his teacher knows he is there, say goodbye to him, then leave the school. Your child will cope perfectly without you; almost certainly his tears will stop within a few moments.

(On the other hand, do not be upset and disappointed if he does not cry. Look on that positively. If your child is well-composed and confident on the first day, then you have prepared him well for school. That is something to be proud of, not something to be depressed about.)

Have your own plan for the day, so that you are kept busy. You may feel slightly down, possibly lonely – that is a perfectly normal reaction when your child starts infant school. Just as your child will find it helpful to have a structured first day at school, so will you.

When you meet him at the end of the day (and every day), let him tell you everything that happened if he wants to. That is the best way to encourage his interest in classroom life, and will help him develop an enthusiasm for school that should stay with him for the rest of his education. Remember, though, that he may be very tired both physically and emotionally by home-time, and that he might not feel like telling you all the details straight away. Be patient, take him home, give him a drink and something to eat, and then let him tell you things in his own time.

THE FOLLOWING DAYS

The next morning should not be so hectic, as long as you have remembered to lay out his clothes, pack his bag, prepare his lunch, and organize any other equipment he needs for the next day. In fact, this should be part of your family's routine from now on during the week. Your child will gradually grow into this routine within a few weeks, and you will find that you spend less time organizing him in the morning. As long as he goes to bed early enough (so that he is not tired when he wakes up) and rises early enough in the morning (so that he does not have a hectic rush to get to school on time), then his morning routine should be relaxed.

You will almost certainly take him to school every day – unless an older sibling takes him, or if he is in a school run – and therefore you do not have to worry too much about his personal safety at this stage. However, this is still a good time to start teaching him how to be streetwise.

The first dimension of becoming streetwise is to learn road safety. He will be taught this in school eventually, but in the mean time you should try to teach him how to be safe from traffic when he is outdoors. The statistics are worrying, because they prove school-aged children are most at risk:

over 20,000 children are either killed or injured on our roads each year, as a result of accidents that could usually have been avoided.

road traffic accidents are the major cause of death among school-aged children, ahead of disease and other causes.

deaths on the road are responsible for up to half of the accidental deaths of children between the ages of 5 and 14 years.

the road accident rate for children between 5 and 9 years is at least four times the road accident rate for adults.

over a fifth of all road accidents involving children aged 5 to 9 years happen during journeys to and from school.

Clearly, your school-aged child is at risk making the trip to school in the morning and returning home at the end of the day. You may be in the fortunate position of being able to take him there and back, though he is unlikely to want to continue with this arrangement once he is settled in the infant class. Or you may have older children who attend the same school and who are prepared to supervise your younger child along the way. However, he still needs to know basic road safety for coping when he is on his own – it could save his life.

One of the factors that puts your child more at risk when crossing the road is that he is small, and this means he is not easily seen by drivers. A waste paper bin on the corner might hide him from view as he waits to cross the road; he may not be tall enough even to rise above the boot of the car he is standing beside. To take into account this lack of height, your child should wear some item of bright clothing (or reflective arm-bands) that distinguishes him from the background, and he should also know not to cross the road between parked cars – explain that he cannot be seen easily.

Another factor that puts your child more at risk in traffic is that 5-year-olds are not very good at looking round before stepping into the road – research studies have found that around half of all children this age do not bother to look for traffic when they start to cross. Frightening, isn't it? Stress to your child that he must pause before moving into the road, that he must look both ways before going any further, and that he should listen for the sound of cars even though he may not be able to see them. If the road is not clear, he should not cross. In the month prior to your child starting the infant class, take him out into the street for practical road-safety lessons with you.

The second dimension of becoming streetwise relates to personal safety. You will probably have talked to him about 'stranger danger' already, but you will certainly need to talk about this with him again, now that he is attending school. Tell your child plainly – but without frightening him – that he must never talk to a stranger, or take sweets from a stranger, or go into a car with a stranger. Make sure he understands that 'bad' people often look the same as 'good' people, so he will not know who is dangerous just by looking at them. Reassure him that you will never reprimand him for refusing to go with an adult he does not know, even, for instance, if you had asked your friend to pick him up from school one day and he would not go with that person because he had not seen her before.

By the time your child reaches school age, he has been encouraged to listen to adults, to be respectful to them and not to draw attention to himself when he is out in public. Yet dealing with stranger danger requires him to do the exact opposite. Tell him that if he feels he is in danger, he should shout out 'Help, help!' and keep shouting until some attends to him. Give him your explicit permission to do this.

SUMMARY

Your child will find the start of school so much easier if he is used to temporary separations from you during the pre-school years, for instance when he attends nursery or playgroup, when he joins a leisure class, or even when you leave him at home with a babysitter. To start with, however, he may find these temporary – yet normal – separations upsetting; that is why you need to have a clear strategy. Tell your child in advance, reassure him that he will be fine, make the separation brief and return on time. The same principles apply when leaving him in the infant school on his first day.

The subsequent days at school will be less hectic than the first day, but you still need to ensure your child is well-organized each night and that he gets up in the morning in plenty of time. Now is the time also to teach him basic road safety and to make him aware of 'stranger danger'.

PROBLEMS IN SCHOOL

11

WHEN THINGS GO WRONG

For many young children the first years in infant school are thoroughly enjoyable, stimulating and rewarding, a time of exciting new experiences and new friends. Yet for other children this same period proves to be difficult and demanding, a time when things go wrong for them.

The range of problems that children can experience at this stage in their lives is diverse. If you discover that your child is having difficulty in the infant school, then tackle it straight away rather than leaving it in the hope that it will go away spontaneously. Fortunately, most childhood problems in school can be resolved if parents and teachers play their parts properly.

'MY CHILD DOESN'T WANT TO GO TO SCHOOL'

Nearly every child is reluctant to go to school sometimes, perhaps because she is tired, wants to avoid a particular lesson, would rather stay at home to watch television, and so on. That is normal. But your child's repeated attempts to avoid going to the infant class are worrying, and should not be ignored. Take her repeated cry 'I don't want to go to school' seriously.

Your first step should be to confirm that she is in good

health. Of course she may tell you she has a sore tummy even though she genuinely feels fine, but on the other hand her sore tummy could be real. Take her temperature and note whether or not she has been vomiting or has had diarrhoea in the past week or so. She may have had headaches too. In most instances, a day or two in bed is enough to ensure speedy recovery from a minor childhood illness. Should the symptoms persist then take your child to her GP for a full medical examination.

If no underlying physical cause is identified, then consider the possibility that your child's discomfort is a psychological reaction to something that is making her unhappy. The list of events that can make a young child unhappy in infant school is endless, but includes:

- falling out with her best friend
- difficulty keeping up with class work
- lack of self-confidence
- being teased about her appearance
- not having the 'right' fashion clothes
- feeling lonely
- bullying and victimization
- inability to find her way round the school
- dislike of the class teacher
- fear of using the school toilets
- dislike of school meals
- poor performance in PE.

Any one of these (or other) concerns may be sufficient to make your child unhappy about going to school. Even though she may not realize the true cause of her distress, you have to do your best to find out what is troubling her:

- **Ask her directly if there is anything upsetting her.** The chances are that she will tell you only that she feels ill, and that she cannot think of anything that she dislikes in school. But have a chat with her about it anyway. Talk with her about the key areas of her school life – e.g. friends, class work, games, playground activities, school meals, school toilets and her teacher.

- **Identify any change in her pattern of behaviour.** When you think carefully you may notice that there has been a change in her behaviour in some way – for instance that she no longer talks about a particular friend anymore, or that she makes only negative comments about her teacher. This can point you to the source of trouble.

- **Talk to her class teacher.** Your child's class teacher is the best source of information regarding her progress in school. Make a special appointment to speak to her, explain your concerns, and listen to her observations. This also serves to bring the teacher's attention to your child's unhappiness, something she may not have been aware of.

- **Make changes where necessary.** Sometimes the problem can be solved quite easily. For instance, a change to another group within the class or additional help from the class teacher for a few days may be all that is needed to make your child more settled. If there is a practical solution like this, then carry it out as soon as you can.

- **Ensure she attends school.** No matter what the problem is, or how long it takes you to resolve it, make sure your child goes to school regularly. The longer she is absent the harder it will be for her to return to a pattern of regular attendance. Take her to school even though she may be tearful, all the time reassuring her that everything will be fine.

Problems at home can be another factor causing her unhappiness. If your child feels insecure about her home life then she may unconsciously be afraid to go to school in case something happens while she is away for the day. Here are some reasons that could make a young child feel insecure about her home life:

- One of her parents is working away from home.

- Someone in the family is seriously ill.

- Her parents fight a lot in front of her.

- There is a new baby in the family.

- A close relative has died recently.

- Her parents are fussy and over-protective.

- Her parents are going through a separation/divorce.

Consider these possibilities if your child complains that she does not want to go to school. The sooner that the root cause of the problem is identified and sorted out, the quicker your child will settle into school once again.

'My Child Finds the Work Too Hard'

Educational surveys reveal that approximately 1 in 5 children in primary school has learning difficulties requiring extra attention from the class teacher. However, in most instances that extra help within the classroom is sufficient to enable the child to progress to the next stage in the curriculum (see Chapter 12 for a fuller discussion of children with special educational needs, i.e. children who have serious and long-term learning difficulties).

Sometimes a child complains that the work in class is too hard simply because she finds it challenging. The strength of a good teacher is the ability to find an educational activity that is sufficiently demanding to interest the child and yet is not so demanding that she gives up too quickly. In the first class in particular, children frequently lack confidence when faced with new learning assignments. If your child does complain like this, boost her confidence by reminding her that she is just as capable as any other child in her class and give her extra help at home.

If the learning problem lasts more than a week or so, speak to her teacher. Do not wait until your child is in tears about her class performance. Explain to the teacher precisely where you think the problem lies (for instance, with reading, addition, writing), and ask for her own opinion on this. Be prepared to listen to what she tells you. Many apparent learning difficulties in the first year at infant school turn out to be temporary (see Chapter 7), despite the initial concern.

Ask the teacher for advice on how you can help your child at home. She may give you short educational tasks for your child after school and, if so, you should carry these out in the way she suggests. You may feel tempted to extend the amount of time your child spends on homework – especially when her progress is slow – by adding on another 30 minutes or even another hour. But this is usually unproductive. For a child aged 5 or 6 years, a short episode of homework lasting 5 to 10 minutes is sufficient once each evening after school. There is absolutely no point in you and your child working together on homework for hour after hour; her concentration will slip after 10 minutes –

and so will your patience.

Having discussed the learning difficulty with the class teacher on the first occasion, set a date (perhaps in three weeks time) to meet the teacher again for further discussion. That provides a point for you all to work towards. Determine what the learning target should be for that meeting (e.g. your child should be able to distinguish between the letters b, p and d). You may have to do this several times during the school year until you are confident that the problem is resolved. However, if the learning targets are not achieved, despite the additional help from the teacher in school and from you at home, then you should raise the issue of further additional learning support for your child.

Most schools have a teacher who has responsibility for providing learning support to pupils with learning difficulties. This may be a promoted teacher or a part-time teacher who only works with children in the school with learning problems. Many local education authorities have a peripatetic learning support service that provides visiting teachers to work directly with pupils who have learning difficulties. Where the difficulty continues to be severe and has been evident for several months, the headteacher might suggest that your child is assessed by the school's educational psychologist in order to pinpoint the exact nature of the learning difficulty (see Chapter 12).

'MY CHILD HATES SCHOOL MEALS'

Lunchtime is such an important part of the school day for your child. It certainly should be a time she looks forward to, and also should be a time when she can relax, satisfy her hunger and have a good chat with her friends. School can seem miserable to a child who does not have a pleasant lunchtime.

There is no reason why your child should not find something on the menu that she likes. Unlike when you were at school, today's dinner ladies offer a range of healthy snacks such as tuna or cheese sandwiches, baked potatoes with a filling, and even pizza. Drinks, too, are varied. So there is bound to be at least one or two items to suit your child. Talk to her about this; you may find she thinks she is not allowed to buy these particular products because she knows you regard them as 'junk food'. Remind your child that she can choose anything she wants to. Encourage her to persist with school meals, if you can.

Small children are often dissuaded from using the school dining hall because it is such a noisy place, with lots of older and bigger children moving around all the time. Fortunately, most infant schools separate younger children from older pupils in the dining hall, so that they are not competing against each other for a place in the queue while waiting to be served. Check with the class teacher that your child's school has this arrangement, and complain if it does not.

The best alternative to school meals is a packed lunch, although this may not be convenient for you, especially when you are rushing off to work in the morning as soon as your child goes to school. However, it does offer her the opportunity to choose her own lunch, thus increasing the likelihood of her eating it. And most young children love having a brightly-coloured lunch box to display to all their friends. Infant schools usually have a separate eating area for children who are having a packed lunch, and it is often quieter than the school dining-hall itself.

'I Want to Teach my Child at Home'

If you want, and if you think you have the necessary skills and educational materials, then current government legislation allows you to teach your child (or organize your child's teaching arrangements) at home. The principal legal authority for this comes from the 1944 Education Act, which states: 'It shall be the duty of the parent of every child of compulsory school age to cause him to receive efficient full-time education suitable to his age, either by regular attendance at school or otherwise.' It is the phrase 'or otherwise' that makes education at home legally possible. In addition, the 1944 Education Act also states: 'Local Authorities shall have regard to the general principle that, so far as is compatible with the provision of suitable instruction and training, and the avoidance of unreasonable expenditure, pupils are to be educated in accordance with the wishes of their parents.' (Although this Act applies only to England and Wales, there are equivalent Acts covering Scotland and Northern Ireland).

No parent takes on this role lightly. However, it is not easy to appreciate the demands of educating your child at home, until you actually embark on the task – and remember that this continues until she is 16 years old or until she returns to a local authority school.

Here are the main requirements when taking responsibility for schooling your child at home:

- a full timetable that approximately matches the number of hours your child would spend in a local authority school

- an academic curriculum that could lead to the standards of literacy and numeracy achieved by the typical local authority school

- a broader curriculum covering such subjects as environmental studies, art, drama, and music

- access to sporting and leisure facilities so that your child can take part in physical activities each week

- a system of recording your child's progress in each subject, and of identifying the next educational targets

- access to all the relevant educational materials involved in delivering this full and broad curriculum at home

- an understanding of teaching skills necessary to educate a child of this age satisfactorily

- an area of the house specifically designated as a study area, so that this can be used as your child's 'school'.

A child who attends school mixes with other children all the time, both socially and educationally. She learns to cooperate with others in classroom activities, to share ideas with other children, and to help other children with their learning. A child who is taught at home does not have these experiences, and therefore it is important to make sure she has social contact with other children her own age during the week.

If you have made up your mind to follow this course of

action, then contact your local Education Department. You should also contact voluntary agencies for help and advice, such as Education Otherwise (see Useful Addresses).

'MY CHILD IS BULLIED'

Bullying is more common in our infant schools than people like to believe. A recent study of several schools found that the number of young children who were bullied varied from none to nearly half the school. On average, almost 30 per cent of the pupils were involved in bullying to some extent, either as bully or victim. Although you may think of bullying at school only in terms of direct physical violence, it can take many forms:

- the use of hands: punching or slapping to the face or body, pushing, nudging or jostling, poking in the side or face, rude gestures

- the use of legs: violent kicking, deliberate tripping, kicking the victim's schoolbag or lunch box, stamping on her foot

- extortion: demanding money from a child, then threatening her with a beating if she does not cooperate fully with these demands

- verbal abuse: teasing a child about her appearance or disability, using words to taunt her, threatening to hurt her

- racial harassment: racially-motivated attacks, either physical or psychological, occurring on or off school premises.

Although bullying is very real and obvious to the child on the receiving end, it may not be obvious to her parents. Often a victim withstands bullying for several months without saying anything about it, because she is afraid that telling her parents will make the bully pick on her even more.

Signs of bullying vary from child to child, and include a fear of going to school, unexplained bruises, cuts, grazes and scratches on her hands, legs and face, regular 'loss' of her schoolbag and lunch box, repeated 'loss' of money for school dinner, and even the occurrence of toilet 'accidents'. None of these signs on its own means that your child is being bullied in school, but you should be aware of the possibility even though your child may not tell you herself. Always be concerned about any uncharacteristic change in your child's behaviour that develops once she has started infant school.

Research has shown that girls are just as likely as boys to experience bullying in school. However, boys tend to be more physically violent when bullying, whereas girls tend to use verbal abuse, teasing and social exclusion. Bear in mind, though, that all types of bullying are painful to the victim.

The prime responsibility for eliminating bullying in the infant school rests with the teachers, and there are plenty of preventative programs for school staff to use with young children. Many infant schools now have a planned, preventative approach to bullying as part of school policy. None of these schemes is guaranteed to have 100 per cent success, but they can create an atmosphere in school that makes bullying unacceptable in the eyes of the pupils.

Always report your child's claims of bullying to the class teacher. You cannot reasonably expect school staff to take action unless they are made aware of the problem. However, your child may insist on a guarantee that the bully will never find out who told the teacher, and if you agree to that, then stick to it – otherwise your child will not trust you enough to confide in you in the future.

Irrespective of the teacher's action against bullying, you can help your child to cope in the following ways:

- **Never make light when she complains of bullying.** It is a serious matter to her, and she needs you to respond positively. The chances are that she will be upset when telling you about it – she is afraid of your reaction. Always reassure her that you will keep the matter confidential if that is what she insists you do.

- **Suggest that she keep a 'low profile' in school.** When in the playground, she should behave in a way that does not attract attention to herself. Sometimes a child who is bullied is loud and outgoing herself, and she receives abuse because the bully feels threatened by her. Your child should stay in the background until the bullying eases.

- **Remind her to stay in safe areas within school.** Most bullying takes place out of sight from teachers, for instance at the hidden end of the playground or behind the coal shed. Your child is less at risk if she avoids these areas and stays closer to the central school building. Some infant schools allow pupils to take their mid-morning break inside the classroom.

- **Persuade her to keep a neutral expression on her face if bullied.** The typical school bully thrives on the fear that she generates in others – it meets her emotional need to be powerful. However, if your child is able to remain calm, without reacting too tearfully, then the bully may decide to leave her alone.

- **Never encourage retaliation.** The responsibility for stopping your child from being bullied rests with you and the class teacher, not with your child. She may not be as strong physically as the bully, so retaliation could backfire. And as well as that, she will be in as serious trouble as the bully if a teacher spots her fighting with another pupil.

- **Suggest she stay in a crowd, when in the playground.** Bullies pick on children who appear weak and isolated – and therefore a child standing alone in a playground is easily identified as a potential target. Being with a crowd does not guarantee an undisturbed playtime, but it does make bullying less likely.

'MY CHILD IS BORED'

A child who is under-stimulated in school will be bored, no matter how much she likes the other children and her teacher. Every child needs to be challenged educationally and intellectually, and the teacher's responsibility is to provide a range of activities and materials that will offer this challenge.

But there are wide individual differences among children starting school. Some have no experience of books, some are able to open a book and look at the pictures, and some already have learned elementary reading skills. Similarly, some children have little idea about counting and numbers, while others are able to carry out simple calculations without any help from the class teacher. In theory the needs of every child should be met in the infant class. In practice, however, few teachers are prepared to provide a separate and individual curriculum for those infants who are already well down the road to mastering the 'three Rs' when they start school.

This means, therefore, that a child who can read and count may become bored after a few weeks in the infant class, simply because she finds the work too easy. If your child makes this complaint to you, check it out. Ask her to give you specific examples of tasks that she claims are too easy for her, and verify for yourself that her assertions are accurate. Monitor the situation for a couple of weeks – you may find that only one or two activities are at too low a level for her, while the rest are ideally suited.

If you are convinced that your child is bored through

lack of challenge, then raise this with her teacher. Explain why you think this and give the teacher lots of examples to support your claim. (Do not be put off by a teacher who tells you have an over-inflated view of your child's ability.) In most instances parents are reassured to hear that the teacher is already aware of the situation and that the child is now working with a small group of children who are all at a similar stage – this is a useful strategy and will soon eliminate boredom.

Ask the teacher for 'extension materials' – work at the level your child can cope with, but varied – so that you can use this with her at home. Rather than accelerating your child through the curriculum, extension materials provide variety at the same level and ensure that your child's learning skills are fully consolidated before she moves on to the next stage.

'MY CHILD IS APATHETIC ABOUT SCHOOL'

Some children are, by nature, withdrawn and passive, showing little enthusiasm for anything. For other children, though, these characteristics signify a deeper unhappiness. Should you discover your child is apathetic, listless and unenthusiastic once she has been attending school for a few months, ask yourself the following questions:

- *How long has she been like this?* Most children are apathetic at some stage in their school life – this is a normal part of child development. But if this pattern persists over a longer period of, say, several months, then there may be something more serious underlying it. Time is an important factor in judging the gravity of your child's behaviour.

- *Has she ever behaved this way before?* Use your knowledge of your child's previous behaviour to decide how significant her current behaviour is. For example, if you know that she is generally unenthusiastic about anything new she tries, then her apathy in the early weeks of infant school is nothing to worry about. It will probably soon pass.

- *Are there any other signs that she is troubled?* A child under stress often displays more than one sign of inner unhappiness. Occasional passivity and apathy are not serious in themselves. However, if that pattern is also accompanied by other signs such as tearfulness, sleeplessness or lack of appetite, then the apathy cannot be dismissed so lightly.

- *Has she changed suddenly?* You need to judge your child's present behaviour in the light of her past behaviour. It is the change in her behaviour which matters, especially if that change is sudden and apparently spontaneous. Unexpected shifts in your child's development are always worthy of your attention and consideration.

- *Have you tried to help your child?* Look for the obvious things that might be linked to her lack of enthusiasm, such as problems with school work or with friends, and try to tackle these. Whatever you do to help your child, carry it out consistently for at least three or four weeks before altering your strategy. Your child needs consistency from you.

- *Is her apathy linked to events outside of her school life?* Of course, you should look closely at your child's progress in school when trying to determine the cause of her apathy. But you should also consider the possibility that the cause of this lies outside school, such as problems at home, difficulties with relationships, and so on. Think about these as well.

There is more to understanding your child's disinterest towards school than simply asking yourself these very basic questions. However, they will point you in the right direction. In most cases you will find that her listlessness and lack of enthusiasm are parts of a passing phase, and that all she needs is encouragement from you.

'MY CHILD HAS NO FRIENDS'

One of the many exciting facets of school life, as far as your child is concerned, is making new friends. She wants to be liked by others, to be included in their games and activities and to be valued by them. Even if she is shy, she still has a need to be accepted by other children her own age. What goes on between your child and her classmates in the playground, in the school corridors and in the classroom itself has a direct effect on her level of enjoyment – if she is lonely with no friends, then she will feel miserable. And many learning activities in school require children to cooperate with each other, and to listen to other points of view.

Numerous studies have shown that a popular child, compared to an unpopular child, tends to be:

- **academically capable: she does well in the infant class, and gains high marks in exams at all stages of school**

- **physically attractive: the more a child's appearance conforms to the prevailing concept of 'good-looking', then the more popular she is likely to be**

- **mature: a child who is physically and emotionally mature tends to be more popular than a less mature child**

- **youngest children: a first-born child is frequently less popular than a youngest child in a family**

- athletic: a child with good sporting ability is more likely to be popular than a physically inept child.

There is little you can do about these qualities – your child either has or has not got these features. However, her popularity also depends on her social skills. Despite an inherent tendency towards social involvement, children still need to learn how to behave in ways that will make them popular. Having these 'social' skills is no guarantee of instant popularity, but they go a long way towards it. The main ones are the ability to communicate effectively, social confidence, the ability to share, take turns and to follow rules, good personal hygiene and acceptable behaviour at mealtimes (see Chapter 5).

'I Don't Like My Child's School Friend'

Think about your own friendships for a few moments. Perhaps you like one of your friends because she is fun-loving and makes you laugh, and perhaps you like another of your friends because she is serious, reliable and trustworthy. Each of your friendships is unique, with its own distinctive characteristics. The same applies to your child and her friendships. Whatever the reason your child has for liking another child, friendships are very important when starting school.

Having friends in school means that she has other children to keep her company when she has time for play, to talk to about what has just happened to her in class, to share all the latest school gossip with, and to help her when she is stuck with something. What you as a mature adult look for in a friendship may well be different from what your child looks for in her friends.

Research studies have shown that school-age children tend to select friends who are:

- of the same sex
- at the same level of emotional and social maturity
- similar in personality characteristics to themselves
- not necessarily as intelligent as themselves.

Other trends have emerged too. For instance, only-children are more capable of sustaining friendships for a longer period than are children from large families; girls appear to be more sociable than boys and find it easier to make friends in school; capable and energetic children rarely select lethargic and unresponsive children to be their friends; friendships among infant schoolchildren change regularly and might not even last for more than a couple of days; friendships are more stable, consistent and durable by the time your child has reached the aged of 10 or 11 years.

You may find, though, that your child becomes friendly with a child that you do not like (because you think she will have a detrimental effect on your child's behaviour and because you dislike the child's parents). Do not create a crisis unnecessarily by reacting too quickly. Take time to decide what you intend to do about this. Much as though you would like to, never forbid your child to play with another child in her class, since this will only have the opposite effect to that you want to achieve – forbidden fruit is always more exciting! Be honest with your child. Tell her what concerns you about the friendship, explaining why you would prefer her to play with another child instead. Do not keep repeating everything you think is wrong with her friend, or your child will consider you are being totally unfair in your judgment. Give a balanced view.

However, schools are small communities, with their own

standards and values. Even though your child may want to please you by not playing any more with this particular child, she might find she has no choice, perhaps because she is not friendly with anyone else or because the child you do not like is exceptionally popular and plays with everyone.

A more positive approach when trying to discourage one friendship is to encourage another. Focus your child's time and attention on an alternative friendship. The younger she is, the easier this is to do. For instance, suggest to your child that she should invite a child from her class (one you do like) to go out with her at the weekend to the park; make the outing sound attractive. In the end your child is still going to make up her own mind about whom she wants to be friendly with, but your persistent attempts to nurture particular friendships may pay off eventually.

'MY CHILD IS OVER-SHADOWED BY HER OLDER BROTHER'

Sibling rivalry – jealousy between brothers and sisters – is found in virtually every family because the children have to share their parents' time, attention, love and money. Jealousy is so destructive, and no child or adult likes to admit the she feels jealous of anyone, let alone of her brothers and sisters. Sibling rivalry can lead to verbal and physical aggression between them.

Starting school can be a potential flashpoint for sibling rivalry, especially for the younger child. Although having an older brother at the same school can be very reassuring for a new infant pupil, it also means that she may well be judged by his previous performance and behaviour. For example, if he is very clever and has made excellent academic achievements, then her performance may be compared to her sibling by teachers, and possibly by your relatives and friends. Not only is this unfair, it is also destructive.

Every child is an individual with her own strengths and weakness, and she should be valued for her individual talents, characteristics and achievements. Comparisons with an older sibling serve no positive purpose. If the comparison is unfavourable (e.g. 'Your brother was able to read much quicker than you when he was your age') then it sets the younger child against the older child, lowers her self-esteem and reduces her enthusiasm for school. And if the comparison is favourable (e.g. 'You are learning so much more than your brother ever did'), then it reflects very badly on the older child and will intensify feelings of sibling rivalry. So make a specific effort to avoid such unproductive comparisons, and speak to the class teacher if you discover she is making comparisons like that in school.

Another way to avoid your younger child being overshadowed by an older sibling is to use their differences in abilities and achievements in a positive way. For example, an older child who is a capable reader can help a younger sibling who is learning to read. Working together like that harnesses the younger child's enthusiasm, makes the older child feel helpful and important, and encourages both children to cooperate with each other.

Sometimes the younger child makes sibling comparisons even though her parents and teachers do not mention it. This is more difficult to tackle because it is generated from the younger child herself. Yet the strategy for tackling it is the same – emphasize the younger child's strengths and her individual talents and achievements. It may be helpful to encourage her to take up a non-academic leisure activity (such as learning to play a musical instrument), as long as it is one her older sibling is not involved in.

Summary

Most problems in the first two years in infant school are minor and can be resolved quite quickly if the responsible adults in her life help the child. If your child complains that she does not want to go to school, or appears unenthusiastic, try to identify the cause of her unhappiness. It could be something at school – or at home – troubling her. Talk to your child about it, and seek advice from her class teacher.

12

CHILDREN WITH SPECIAL NEEDS

Every child with special needs is different, and should be treated as an individual. The term 'special needs' covers a wide range of developmental conditions in childhood, including general problems such as slowness learning to talk and limited understanding, genetic problems such as Down's syndrome and Fragile-X syndrome, sensory problems such as partial sight or partial hearing, and physical problems such as spina bifida and cerebral palsy.

A child with special needs has the same psychological needs as any other child. For example, he still has the need to be loved by his parents, the need to be accepted by his peers, the need to make achievements in school, and so on. However, his developmental difficulty means that he also has special needs in addition to these. For example, a child with a physical disability might need to have toys brought to him because he cannot move across the room to reach them, and a child with Down's syndrome might have difficulties with concentration.

And there are likely to be special educational needs when the child starts nursery or infant school, when he begins to experience new learning challenges. He may not be able to learn at the same rate as the other children his age, or he may require a higher level of supervision in the infant class. A child with a physical disability often requires special practical arrangements in infant school, such as ramps to allow him full access round the building.

Preparing your child with special needs for school is a demanding challenge for you. As with every child, however, there is plenty that you can do to help his development during the pre-school years.

PLAY FOR CHILDREN WITH SPECIAL NEEDS: BIRTH–3 YEARS

Play is as important for your child with special needs as it is for your other children – it remains his natural medium for learning, even though he has developmental difficulties. But the problem with some children who have special needs is that they tend to be passive rather than active explorers. He may, for instance, not be particularly motivated to reach out and touch toys that are laid beside him. And he may not seem interested in examining a toy once he has it in his grasp. However, this only proves that you need to work harder with him in order to stimulate his play activities.

Here are some reasons why a child with special needs often requires more encouragement to play:

- **hand-eye coordination problems.** His hand and finger control might be weak, which means that he cannot manipulate toys as easily as other children. Small items will be hard for him to handle and he might not be able to guide his hands in the desired direction. He will soon lose interest if he cannot hold the toy properly.

- **not fully understanding about cause-and-effect.** His limited understanding of the world also applies to his understanding of toys. Unlike your other children when they were that age, your child with special needs might not realize that the light went on because he activated the switch when he pushed the button. He does not see the significance of his actions in play.

- **unsuitable toys.** Do not buy fancy electronic toys in the hope that this will encourage his learning – they may be so sophisticated that he gives up instantly. Instead, buy him toys that are appropriate for his level of understanding at the time. It comes down to knowing your child well so that you can select a toy that will attract his attention.

- **adults who are too helpful.** Most people have difficulty watching a child with special needs struggling, for instance, to put one block on top of the other, and want to help him by putting the block on for him. But this simply leads him to expect that others will always sort out his toys and games for him. Too much help when playing encourages his passivity.

If your child does have special needs, here are some suggestions for encouraging him to play:

- **Accept that passivity may be part of your child's condition.** Try not to become frustrated when you see him lying in his cot apparently doing absolutely nothing, or sitting in his high chair staring blankly at the toys on the tray in front of him without actually touching any of them. Instead, start the play process off, perhaps by taking the toy to him or by placing his hands round the toy. He will benefit from this type of prompting.

- **Pick toys and games according to his level of development, not according to his age.** Much as though you might like him to be able to play with a toy that is popular with children his age, he will not be able to make sense of it unless he has a similar level of understanding. Be prepared to buy him toys that are normally associated with younger children.

- **Expect slow progress.** You will probably find that he likes to play with a toy long after you expected him to lose interest. He needs more time than other children to learn all that he can from a toy, so he plays with it for longer. Similarly, his next toy should not be too challenging for him or he will not be motivated to play with it. Progress will be slow, but that should not keep you or your child from taking pleasure from his play activities.

- **Do not drive him too hard.** Of course he needs your encouragement to learn, and of course he needs you to suggest that he tries that bit harder to complete the inset board or jigsaw puzzle. But remember that he is probably doing the best he can – he would love to be able to solve the puzzle more quickly. He will switch off completely if he feels his efforts are undervalued by you, or that you are pressurizing him too much.

- **Be patient and optimistic.** Your child will become demotivated if he thinks you are disappointed in him and in his play achievements. He wants to see a big smile on your face when he shows you that he has just drawn something on a piece of paper – he does not want you to look glumly at him because you had hoped for more. Take the attitude that he is going to progress, and that his play patterns will mature in time.

- **Help him out at times.** There is absolutely no point in letting him struggle to complete a game for hour after hour. Success motivates, failure depresses. So help him out. You probably will not have to do it all for him, but you should at least start him off on the right road towards the solution. You can also show him different ways of playing with same toy, for example by demonstrating that a ball can be bounced as well as rolled, that it can be thrown as well as kicked.

Your child with special needs probably does not need special toys, especially during the first 3 years. (If he does, say because he has particular balance or mobility difficulties, then you will be given advice from the specialists who are involved with your child). He will enjoy the same range of toys as any other child, except that he may prefer items that are popular with a younger age group. You need look no further than your local toy shop at this stage.

RAISING YOUR CHILD WITH SPECIAL NEEDS

The following 10-Point Action Plan may be helpful for raising your child with special needs during the pre-school years:

1. **Accept unpredictability.** Nobody can tell you exactly what your child will be like when he is 5 years old, or what problems he will face when starting school. And the younger he is at the time, the less accurate will be the predictions. The effect of this is that you will have to live with a great deal of uncertainty during the early years of your child's life.

2. **Learn about your child's condition.** Lack of knowledge can be frightening, especially when your child has a problem that you know very little about. So gather as much information as you can about his difficulty from the doctors, psychologists and teachers that your child becomes involved with. You will be able to find leaflets and books in your local library.

3. **Speak to other parents who are in a similar situation.** You will probably feel better talking to other parents who have had the same experience as you. Hearing their accounts of the challenges of raising a child with special needs may reassure you, and may be a useful source of support and advice. Your local child development clinic can put you in touch with other parents.

4. **Ask lots of questions.** Your child will be seen by a variety of professionals during the pre-school years, each examining and assessing him from a different perspective. You should know their findings. Parents with a child who has special needs often feel that they get fobbed off by professionals when they ask a question. Do not let that happen – keep asking.

5. **Respond to your child's emotional needs too.** Life with a young child who has a developmental difficulty is very busy. Hospital and clinic appointments take up much of your time. But do not forget that it is difficult for him too. Amid all the practical arrangements, make time for you and him to be together, enjoying each other's company. He needs that too.

6. **Have the same standards of discipline for all your children.** Your child with special needs requires consistency at home, as do all your other children. Different expectations and standards of behaviour for a child with special needs confuse him, and will encourage him to develop a self-image in which he perceives himself as different from his brothers and sisters.

7. **Expect the best of your child with special needs.** Your child's special needs limit the potential achievements he can make, when compared to other children his own age. However, he should still be encouraged to try hard at every educational and leisure activity he participates in. Aim to develop his skills in every area of his life.

8. **Encourage him to play with other children his own age.** Just because your child has special needs does not mean that he always wants to play with other children who have developmental problems. He should be encouraged to mix with other children his age, at parent-and-toddler group, playgroup and nursery. These opportunities will advance his learning.

9. **Go elsewhere if you are unhappy.** Your natural tendency will usually be to continue with the professionals who first become involved in supervising your child's development, even though you may be dissatisfied with their performance. However, you should consider asking for a referral elsewhere, or for a second opinion, if you are unhappy with them.

10. **Do not turn your child's disability into a handicap.** There are plenty of children with disabilities who lead a normal life. For instance, a child who has a learning difficulty could go out at weekends with his friends, join his local cub group, and so on. Yet if his parents are too restrictive they will keep him at home most of the time – and that could transform his disability into a handicap.

SCHOOLING FOR YOUR CHILD WITH SPECIAL NEEDS

Until recently, most children with special educational needs were expected (often against parental wishes) to attend segregated special schools. The assumed benefits of such schools included:

- smaller classes, with perhaps eight pupils per teacher, compared to perhaps 30 or more pupils per teacher in the local school

- teachers who had undergone further training in teaching methods suitable for children who have special needs

- auxiliary staff, who were readily available to help the children in the classroom, to take them to the toilet and to help them at mealtimes

- access to other essential non-teaching resources, such as in-school speech therapy, physiotherapy and occupational therapy

- individualized educational programs designed to meet each child's individual educational needs

However, questions about the effectiveness of such schools have been raised, and the assumed benefits have been challenged because:

- There is little research evidence which proves that special schools give pupils improved educational results.

- There are many children in their local primary schools who also receive an individualized educational programme.

- Auxiliary staff, and staff providing supportive therapies, can be located in local schools in the same as they can be in special schools.

- Children who attend special schools often have social difficulties later in life because they have lived in such a sheltered environment.

As a result, the trend towards special education in the form of segregated special schools has weakened greatly. Now, many educational professionals support the view that a child with special needs should be integrated into his local school, before considering the possibility of segregated special school. There are three levels of integration:

1. **locational integration.** This type of integration is very basic and simply means that a child with special needs attends his local school, or attends a special class in his local school. But it is integration in name only. In reality the pupil with special needs does not see the other pupils in the school, follows an entirely different curriculum and uses separate play and leisure areas in the school. This might be called integration, but it is not genuine integration.

2. **social integration.** This type of integration is one stage further. As well as attending his local school (or special unit within his local school), a child with special needs mixes socially with the other pupils there. There may be formal arrangements when children with special needs and the other pupils share joint activities such as PE, and they also mix together in the school playground. However, the child with special needs is in a different class.

3. **functional integration.** This type of integration is the ideal standard (which can be achieved with planning, resources and effort) for a child with special needs. He attends the age-appropriate class at his local school, along with all the other children from the neighbourhood. He plays with them and sits alongside them in the classroom. His curriculum will be individualized to meet his special educational needs, but he functions like any other pupil.

Of course, there are some children whose development is so severely impaired, to the point where they require constant care, that their needs cannot be met in an ordinary school. For them, integration is not feasible. However, there is an increasing awareness that many children with special needs can cope in their local school as long as they are given the necessary support and adequate resources. Most local education authorities accept this principle of integration, and are increasingly willing to support pupils with special needs in local schools. For example, in the past children with Down's Syndrome were automatically placed in special schools; now there are many instances of children with Down's Syndrome being educated in their local school. And they are making progress. Some local authorities even start the process of integration at the nursery stage, which makes integration at the infant stage easier.

The choice is yours. Your child will not be integrated into his local school against your wishes, and you will be fully consulted every step of the way. Some parents find the prospect of integration too daunting, as they are afraid their child will lose out on the special resources that he needs, and they opt for his placement in a segregated special school. You have to decide. Fortunately, you are now in a position of having more choice, instead of having a decision for a segregated school made for you by the local authority without consultation.

THE EDUCATION ACT 1981

Get to know the laws that cover the education of children with special needs. You need to know your rights, and your child's rights, before you can best assess what to do. The main Act of legislation that you should be familiar with is the Education Act 1981, along with the Education (Special Educational Needs) Regulations 1983, that came into force in April 1983. (In Scotland, the equivalent legislation is the Education [Scotland] Act 1981).

The Education Act 1981 abolished the previous system of classifying children according to their handicap, and replaces this with the concept of 'special educational needs'. The Act states that 'a child has "special educational needs" if he has a learning difficulty which calls for special educational provision to be made for him' and explains that 'a child has a "learning difficulty" if (a) he has significantly greater difficulty in learning than the majority of children his age; or (b) he has a disability which either prevents or hinders him from making use of educational facilities of a kind generally provided in school, within the area of the local authority concerned, for children of his age.'

Under this Act, local education authorities have a statutory duty to ensure that 'special educational provision is made for pupils who have special educational needs' (and now also for pre-school children aged 2 years or older). In addition, the Act requires local authorities to identify and assess children with special educational needs. However, if the local authority proposes to assess a child's educational needs, it must write to the parents explaining that an assessment is planned, how it will be carried out, and the name of someone in the local authority who can be contacted for further information. The local authority is allowed to seek any advice whatsoever when assessing a child's special educational needs, and all this information is usually gathered by the educational psychologist.

The Statement

In England and Wales, the next stage in this part of the assessment is the preparation and compilation of a Statement of Special Educational Needs – a written account of the child's special educational needs, and the measures that the local authority intends to provide in order to meet these needs. (In Scotland, the equivalent document is known as a Record of Needs.) The design of the Statement may vary from authority to authority, but the content is clearly defined in the Education Act 1981 and in the Special Needs Regulations 1983, and does not vary.

Every Statement is in five sections:

- Part 1: This is an introductory page that sets out all the relevant factual details (name, address, age, name of parent/guardian, etc.) about the child who is the subject of the Statement.

- Part 2: In this section there is a description of the child's special educational needs, as identified by those professionals who have participated in the assessment.

- Part 3: This specifies the educational provision considered necessary to meet the child's special educational needs, and details any facilities, teaching arrangements, curriculum and equipment needed.

- Part 4: This part indicates the type of school thought to be appropriate for the child, or the provision to be made if a child is to attend an establishment other than a school (e.g. hospital). The school can be named.

- Part 5: Details of non-educational provision, considered necessary to enable the child to benefit from the proposed special educational provision, are given here. This would be made available by a health authority.

The draft version of the Statement is sent to the parents along with an explanation of their rights of appeal; if the parents accept the contents of the Statement, then it becomes final. However, there are several ways in which the content of the draft Statement can be challenged (e.g. regarding the provision listed), and the legislation sets out the channels for processing such appeals. The final stage of any appeal – assuming it has not been resolved at an earlier stage – is the Secretary of State – and that minister's decision is binding on the parents and the local education authority.

Coping with Statementing

The process of Statementing is clear, precise and follows a step-by-step sequence. In theory, everything should go according to plan. In practice, however, parents can feel dissatisfied and disempowered by the system of assessment and administration. Common problems reported by parents whose children have been assessed as having special educational needs include lack of consultation (even though the legislation is specifically designed to encourage parental involvement), lack of information about the assessment, professionals who see the child without informing the parents, and lengthy delays in opening a Statement. However, many parents view the experience as helpful and positive.

The chart below offers advice to help reduce your potential anxieties and confusion if your child is identified and assessed as having special educational needs and if a Statement of Special Educational Need is suggested, either at the pre-school stage or when he attends infant school:

What to Do	Explanation
Raise concerns.	Speak to your child's class teacher as soon as you realize he has serious difficulties. Learning problems are best identified sooner rather than later so additional help can be give right away.
Know the legislation.	Read the regulations regarding children who have special educational needs; that is the best way to protect your child's rights. You should get your own copy of the relevant Acts.

Take advice.   Try to listen to professional opinions, without dismissing them out of hand simply because you do not like what you hear. If possible, be unbiased about the results of your child's assessments.

Say what you think.   The legislation governing children with special needs aims to involve parents . You should feel able to say what you think, and to have these views taken seriously.

Have confidence.   Local education authority staff work in a way that is designed to help your child. They want the assessment process to go smoothly, because without your support the child will lose out.

Challenge.   Just because someone is well trained in assessing children's learning difficulties, this does not mean he or she is always right. Ask questions if you do not understand the specialist's opinion.

Complain.   Nobody should see your child for the purpose of assessing his special educational needs without telling you first. If you are not informed in advance, then make a fuss about it.

Visit the provision. You should have an opportunity to visit any school or special resource that might be suitable for your child before agreeing to it. If nobody suggests a visit, then suggest it yourself.

Make contact.   The first letter you receive from your local authority about a Statement for your child will name someone in the authority who will act as your point of contact during the process. Use this contact if you wish.

SUMMARY

For a child with special needs, starting school can be particularly challenging. You can help boost his development during the pre-school years by encouraging his play activities. When raising your child with special needs, find out as much as you can about his difficulty, and speak to other parents who have a child with similar difficulties. Remember that your child has emotional needs too.

Many children with special needs attend their local infant school nowadays, instead of a special school. This is your choice. The Education Act 1981 lays down procedures for assessing and supporting children with special needs, and specifies that a child with special educational needs should have a Statement. The process of opening a Statement is less confusing and stressful for parents when they are informed about the legislation and are prepared to ask questions.

USEFUL ADDRESSES

ADVISORY CENTRE FOR EDUCATION

18 Victoria Park Square
London E2 9PB
(0181–980 4596)

ASSOCIATION FOR POST-NATAL ILLNESS

25 Jerdan Place
London SW6 1BE
(0171–386 0868)

COUNCIL FOR AWARDS IN CHILDREN'S CARE AND EDUCATION

8 Chequer Street
St Albans
Herts AL1 3XZ
(01727 847636)

DOWN'S SYNDROME ASSOCIATION

153–155 Mitcham Road
London SW17 9PG
(0181–682 4001)

DYSLEXIA INSTITUTE

133 Gresham Road
Staines
Middlesex TW18 2AJ
(01784 463851)

EDUCATION OTHERWISE

36 Kinross Road
Leamington Spa
Warwickshire CV32 7EF
(01926 886828)

GINGERBREAD (ASSOCIATION FOR ONE-PARENT FAMILIES)

35 Wellington Street
London WC2E 7BN
(0171–240 0953)

NATIONAL ASSOCIATION FOR GIFTED CHILDREN

Nene College
Park Campus
Broughton Green Road
Northampton NN2 7AL
(01604 792300)

NATIONAL CHILDMINDING ASSOCIATION

8 Masons Hill
Bromley
Kent BR2 9EY
(0181–464 6164)

NATIONAL COUNCIL FOR ONE-PARENT FAMILIES

255 Kentish Town Road
London NW5 2LX
(0171–267 1361)

NATIONAL TOY LIBRARIES ASSOCIATION

(Play Matters)
68 Churchway
London NW1 1LT
(0171–387 9592)

PARENTS AT WORK

77 Holloway Road
London N7 8JZ
(0171–700 5771)

PRE-SCHOOL PLAYGROUP ASSOCIATIONS

61–63 King's Cross Road
London WC1X 9LL
(0171–833 0991)

INDEX

aggression 54-6, 68-71

bullying 148-51

childminders 17
concentration 77-9, 81
confidence 47-9, 65-6
coordination:
  general 28, 30, 33
  hand-eye 29, 31, 33

development:
  birth to 3 years 4-5
  4 years 30-32
  5 years 32-5
  checklist 28-9
  see also coordination;
    intelligence; language
    development; social
    development
discipline 61-2, 165
dyslexia 91-3

eating:
  habits 67-8
  school meals 144-6
education at home 146-8
emotional development see
    social development;
    personality

friendships see school
    problems, friendships;
    social development

independence:
  encouraging 62-4
  goals 58-60
  parental attitudes 61-2
  social 65-8
inquisitiveness 51-2
integration see special needs

language development 28-9,
    31, 33-4 see also thinking

skills, checklist; reading,
pre-reading activities
learning skills *see* thinking
skills
learning style 85-7
left-handedness 96-7
listening skills 49-50

memory:
adult and child 82-3
improving 83-5
short-term and long-term
80-2

nannies 17
number concept:
development of 97-9
pre-number activities
99-100
problems 100-1
nursery:
starting 126 *see also* school,
starting
types of 15-16
choosing 18-22

personality 43-4
play:
creative 7
discovery 5-6
encouraging 0-12 months
8-9
encouraging 12-24 months
9-10

encouraging 24-36 months
10-11
imaginative 7
physical 6
pre-school years 5-8
social 7-8
see also special needs
playgroups:
choosing 18-22
structure of 16-17
positive attitude 45-7
pre-school facilities 15-18

reading:
development of 88-9
pre-reading activities 89-90
problems 91-3
see also dyslexia
respect for others 52-4
road safety 133-5
rules 67

school, choosing:
background information
106-8
local schools 106
visiting 108-13
school, private 114-15
school problems:
anxiety 139-42
apathy 152-4
boredom 151-2
educational 142-4
friendships 154-7

meals 144-6
siblings 157-8
see also special needs
school, readiness for:
curriculum 36
development, 4 years 30-32
development, 5 years 32-5
encouraging 35-9
expectations 37
pupils 37-8
routine 38-9
teachers 37-8
transition 25-8
school building 35-6
see also thinking skills
school, starting:
countdown 119-22
first day 131-3
planning 123-4
preparation 129-31
separation from parent 125-9
sharing 66
siblings 106, 157-8
social development 29, 32, 34
see also aggression;
independence, social;
play, social; respect for
others; school problems,
friendships

special needs:
Education Act 1981, 169-71
integration 168
parenting 164-6
play 0-3 years 161-4
schooling 166-9
Statementing *see* Statement
of Special Educational
Needs
starting school *see* school,
starting
Statement of Special
Educational Needs
coping 170-4
structure 170-2
strangers 135-6

thinking skills:
checklist 74-5
encouraging 75-7
origins 73-4
see also concentration;
learning style; memory
turn-taking 66-7

writing:
development of 93-4
pre-writing activities 94-6
problems 96-7